The **NON-OBVIOUS GUIDE TO**

Being More Creative

(No Matter Where You Work)

ALSO BY KATHRYN P. HAYDON

What Do Birds Say to the Moon?

Creativity for Everybody

*Discovering and Developing Talents
in Spanish-Speaking Students*

OTHER NON-OBVIOUS GUIDES:

The Non-Obvious Guide To Small Business Marketing

The Non-Obvious Guide To Employee Engagement

The Non-Obvious Guide To Event Planning

The Non-Obvious Guide To Emotional Intelligence

PRAISE FOR THE NON-OBVIOUS GUIDE
TO BEING MORE CREATIVE

"This book is a must-read for anyone looking to transform the sluggish inertia of no into the exhilarating momentum of yes. Creativity is not just for self-appointed artists, it is for all of us. The spark of your inner five-year-old awaits. Perhaps it's perfect timing that you've found this book! Kathryn's heart-centered approach radiates on every page with encouragement and enthusiasm. This book will quickly become a go-to guide for all of us to harness exploration, play, personalization, and more joyful possibility in life and work."

—Jenny Blake, Author, *Pivot: The Only Move
That Matters Is Your Next One*

"Uncork all those ideas you've got bottled up inside you with this smart and engaging guide. You'll understand where creativity comes from, what stands in its way (Hello, Impostor Syndrome!), and how to engender creativity in others. Any innovation starts with taking a risk, so take a risk on this book. It will pay off in creative dividends."

— Daniel Pink, Author, *When, Drive,* and *A Whole New Mind*

"The tools and strategies in this book help you take your creative thinking to the next level, to be more consistent and deliberate about using thinking practices that elicit new ideas and result in valuable solutions."

—Dorie Clark, Author of *Reinventing You* and *Stand Out*, and Executive
Education Faculty, Duke University Fuqua School of Business

"Kathryn truly understands what is important in nurturing creativity. She lives with the guiding principle that creativity serves a valuable purpose and she demands results throughout the creative journey."

—John Anderson, Founder and President, JCA Electronics

"As problems in the world mount, creative problem solving becomes an even more valuable skill. This book is a roadmap through the research and practice of maximizing your creativity and crushing your biggest barrier to more innovative work."

—David Burkus, Author, *Under New Management*

"To be successful, a company must bring the next new solution, product, or service to the market first. Organizations that cannot do this quickly become obsolete. How do you help all of your employees to harness their innate ability to think beyond what presently exists and have the confidence to identify the next breakthrough idea? This easy-to-read book lays out the steps and includes relatable, real-life stories. A must-have guide!"

—Susan Youngblood, Global Head of People, Customer Operations, Refinitiv (former Thomson Reuters Financial & Risk)

"In her professional trainings, Kathryn Haydon has inspired our team beyond expectations. This book shares many of the key principles that have helped us grow our creative impact. They will be game-changing for you, too."

—Miles Cameron, Director of Innovation, Rippowam Cisqua School

"When I began to collaborate with Kathryn to apply her creativity and innovation insights to franchising, I learned what creativity really means and how it applies to so many situations and applications throughout business. This book provides ways to innovate, including case studies and tools to implement solutions and measure results. Kathryn helps people achieve their full potential as creative thinkers by activating their untapped strengths so they can do their best work."

—Ab Igram, Managing Director, Head of Franchise, Webster Bank

The **NON-OBVIOUS**
GUIDE TO

Being More Creative

(No Matter Where You Work)

By **KATHRYN P. HAYDON**

IDEAPRESS
PUBLISHING

IDEAPRESS
PUBLISHING

Published in the United States by Ideapress Publishing.

IDEAPRESS PUBLISHING | WWW.IDEAPRESSPUBLISHING.COM

All trademarks are the property of their respective companies.

COVER DESIGN BY JOCELYN MANDRYK

Cataloging-in-Publication Data is on file with the Library of Congress.
ISBN: 978-1940858-92-0

PROUDLY PRINTED IN THE USA

SPECIAL SALES

Ideapress Books are available at a special discount for bulk purchases, for sales promotions and premiums, or for use in corporate training programs. Special editions, including personalized covers, a custom foreword, corporate imprints, and bonus content are also available.

Non-Obvious® is a registered trademark of the Influential Marketing Group.

DEDICATION

To those who have committed their lives to
understanding creativity.

Read this book to find opportunities where no one else sees them. Learn to transform ideas into valuable solutions. Harness your full thinking capacity at work and beyond with creativity—the future survival skill that you need now.

Contents /

PART 2 – HOW TO FOSTER A CREATIVE ENVIRONMENT

→ On Being Humble

→ What If You Get Stuck?

→ Ready, Go!

Is This Guide for You?

If you picked up this book, you are not a dummy.

Many business guides treat you like an idiot. Some even say so on the cover. This is not one of those books.

The **Non-Obvious Guides** all focus on sharing advice that you haven't heard before. Creativity is a big topic and Kathryn was the perfect choice to tackle it for our series. In her guide you'll get amazing practical suggestions for how to harness your own creativity along with suggestions for silencing that inner critic holding you back from doing your best work.

Creativity doesn't have to be scary, or just reserved for people who describe themselves as "artistic." We all have the power to be more creative, and this wonderfully written guide will show you exactly how to do it!

Rohit Bhargava
Founder, *Non-Obvious Guides*

How to Read This Book

Throughout this book you will find links to helpful guides and resources online.

DOWNLOAD LINK:
www.sparkitivity.com/nonobviousresources

Referenced in the book, you will also see these symbols which refer to content that will further your learning.

FOLLOW THE ICONS:

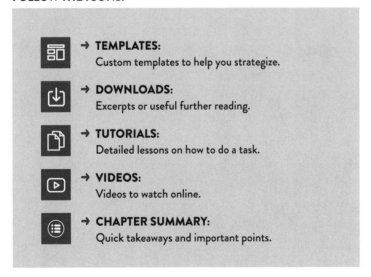

→ **TEMPLATES:**
Custom templates to help you strategize.

→ **DOWNLOADS:**
Excerpts or useful further reading.

→ **TUTORIALS:**
Detailed lessons on how to do a task.

→ **VIDEOS:**
Videos to watch online.

→ **CHAPTER SUMMARY:**
Quick takeaways and important points.

In this book, you will learn to harness your creativity so you can...

→ Think more powerfully and originally.

→ Solve problems more effectively.

→ Give feedback that leads to innovation.

→ Spot thinking strengths in yourself and others.

→ Leverage change to your advantage.

→ Turn problems into possibilities.

→ Ask questions that lead to valuable solutions.

→ Make meetings more productive.

→ Get inspired to do your best work.

Why I No Longer Buy High Heels

The other night I was giving a speech and running up and down the auditorium steps wearing black ankle boots that could have been a medieval torture device.

After the event, I realized I would have to subject myself to another form of torture to fix the problem: shoe shopping.

While I don't mind clothes shopping, I tend to dread shoe shopping because no matter what I do, it feels nearly impossible to get a pair of comfortable, fashionable shoes.

So there I was, stuck driving to the mall on a gorgeous Saturday afternoon to conduct another search (probably in vain) for a pair of good-looking and comfortable shoes for a keynote the following week.

Knowing my style, I loaded my arms with floor samples of the typical high-heeled choices as I canvassed the shoe department with low expectations.

BEING OPEN TO THE CRAZY

My fate changed when I met a salesperson named André-Paul Chin. He was dressed in a bright purple shirt and had a trace of a Jamaican accent. André-Paul was funny, thoughtful, and cheerful as he dutifully brought me one uncomfortable pair of shoes after another.

"I wish the question weren't, 'Which shoe will hurt the least?'" I remarked cynically.

Seeing my frustration, he pointed to his own feet and his trendy, comfortable-looking kicks, and explained how he had stopped wearing dress shoes last year.

"I decided not to suffer anymore, climbing stairs to retrieve boxes of shoes all day long. I went out and found a working shoe to take the place of every dress shoe," André-Paul told me.

I sighed. "I wish I could do that," I said, dismissing the thought. But then he said he had a crazy idea.

He popped open a new box and proceeded to slide a pair of slippers onto my feet. The familiar sheepskin felt heavenly after all of those uncomfortable boots, and we had a good laugh about what might happen if I wore those onstage.

However, wearing that "ridiculous" choice of slippers got me thinking in a new way.

Looking at André-Paul, I asked if he had any more unusual ideas.

Clearly it was the question he was waiting for, because his eyes lit up and he walked me to a table of sparkling, colorful, non-heeled possibilities. A tentative wave of rebellious excitement passed over me as he spoke.

"Why not make shoes your thing?" he asked. "Why not create your own style?"

To bring his suggestion back to reality, he promptly brought out boxes and boxes of eclectic designer sneakers inspired by Italian streetwear. Skater shoes, actually.

All the while, he talked to me about starting a collection. Buying a new pair every month. Surprising audiences with different, wild shoes each time.

"No one will know what you're going to show up in next!"

Clearly André-Paul was a gifted salesperson.

But the possibility he was raising—that maybe, just maybe, I could forevermore work in comfort and create a signature style for myself—felt exciting.

I began picturing my future self on stage with a collection of very expensive skater shoes. It was a major stretch.

I started my career working for a bank when men and women both wore suits. I remember hearing once that there was even an employee whose job it was to measure the hems of women's skirts to ensure they weren't too short. I believed it.

Yet despite my long-held bias about what it meant to dress "professionally," I decided to put my hesitation aside and buy a pair of those shoes.

I'll admit that I had to think twice when getting dressed for that next keynote. But I took the risk and wore the shoes. During the talk I practically floated around the room, weaving without fear of catching a heel among the dozens of tables as I spoke.

Afterward, a crush of women came running up to me. "Thank you for wearing those shoes!" they exclaimed, almost in unison.

As it turns out, other people had the same shoe problem I did.

By going out on a limb and doing something different to solve it, I paved the way to help them find a solution, too.

WHY IT STARTS WITH TAKING A RISK

Of course, this book isn't about buying a different pair of shoes. Or succumbing to the charm of a friendly and effective salesperson.

It is about being willing to take a risk that can open your mind to being more creative.

Sometimes all you need is a gentle nudge from a guide like André-Paul, showing you the path.

The aim of this book is to be that nudge.

In the coming chapters, you will learn how to harness your creativity using the same methods that have worked for thousands of professionals I have had the honor of mentoring and coaching.

André-Paul Chin

The curated collection of tools and techniques I share in this guide will help you adopt a mindset that helps you break through what I call "the inertia of no" (more on that later).

Above all, you will understand how thinking creatively can help you overcome limiting assumptions and do what both André-Paul and I did in that moment back at that shoe store.

WHAT NORDSTROM KNOWS ABOUT CREATIVITY

André-Paul's choice to change his footwear forced him not only to change his mindset but to navigate the corporate culture at a large retailer that could have immediately dismissed his idea.

In a "culture of no" he might never have attempted to make this change, anticipating that it would be shot down. But when the managers at Nordstrom were open to André-Paul's slight shift in dress code so that he could better serve customers and therefore make more sales, they sent a signal and reaffirmed creativity as part of the store culture.

His managers' acceptance signaled that seeking new possibilities was welcome.

They were open to new ideas and willing to be flexible to help employees do their best work.

What if you could work at a place like that?

What if you could be a person like that?

You can, and this book will show you how.

PART ONE

How To Be A Creative Person

CHAPTER 1

What is Creativity?

Can you imagine Albert Einstein sitting at the kitchen table doing a project with glitter and felt?

In the meme that's in my head, he frowns as he struggles to trace the shape shown in the instructions with a thick, black Sharpie. The thought bubble over his wild hair reads, "I guess I'm not creative. I don't like crafts."

But we know Einstein was highly creative. We can also be fairly certain he didn't engage in many do-it-yourself craft projects.

So even if we've used the words "artistic" and "creative" interchangeably before, this example makes it clear that they are not synonymous.

 ## 1.1   Begin with What Bothers You

Let's explore what Einstein did do.

He began with what bothered him.

He spotted problems. He sensed gaps in present knowledge. Then he used his imagination to think beyond accepted assumptions and introduce new ideas.

Thinking differently is another way to describe creativity, and you don't need to be Einstein to do it.

Here are three exercises to help you get started:

Exercise 1 **MAKE A BUG LIST**

What are the things that bother you on a day-to-day basis?

These might be simple items in your daily personal routine, observations you make in your community, or aspects of work. Jot down five or ten of these annoyances. As you read this book, you'll learn tools and techniques to help you think differently enough to turn them into opportunities.

Exercise 2 **PRACTICE BREAKING THROUGH ASSUMPTIONS**

A big part of creativity is learning to spot and think past deeply entrenched assumptions. One tool I use is Nathan Levy's *Stories With Holes* which are like 20 Questions games to help us break through false assumptions. Each "story" is essentially a riddle. Here's an example:

The Masked Man

The man was afraid to go home, because the man with the mask was there.

That's it. The above sentence is the story that needs to be solved.

To play, one person knows the answer. Everyone else asks as many yes or no questions as they need to solve it:

Is the man with the mask a thief? (No.)

Is the man in danger? (No.)

Was the man with the mask in the guy's house? (No.)

Keep asking questions and soon you'll be able to fill in the details to explain the context of this short story. As you can see, there are a lot of assumptions that must be overcome to do so.

(The solution to The Masked Man is in the endnotes so you can try it for yourself!)[1]

Exercise 3 **PLAY MONKEY IN THE MIDDLE**

Can you solve these visual word pictures, sometimes called rebus puzzles?

MIDMONKEYDLE

MILONELION

DAYSALLWORK

T
O
W
N

WEAR
LONG

To solve them, you have to do mental gymnastics to bend and reconnect words, concepts, and visuals in different ways. Search "rebus puzzles" online for more. Once you get the hang of it, make up your own.

(Answers: Monkey in the middle, One in a million, All in a day's work, Downtown, Long underwear).

1.2 Definitions to Understand Creativity

"All models are wrong but some are useful."

- George Box

If you delve into academic research on creativity, you'll find that creativity is often defined as "solving problems in novel and useful ways."

This is a simple, clear, and actionable definition. I like it very much and have used it often in my work.

Yet, creativity isn't always about solving problems. A large part of it is keeping open to opportunities in the face of constant inertia to stay the same.

In this book we will focus on the action of individual creativity in day-to-day work life.

> **Definition:** **INERTIA OF NO**
>
> inertia (n.): the tendency to do nothing or to remain unchanged; resistance to motion, action, or change
>
> inertia of no (n.): limitations such as beliefs, statements, or assumptions that impede thinking, opportunities, or action for progress

In this book, I prefer the following definition of creativity because it helps capture some of the robustness of the term and provides non-obvious insights:

Creativity is breaking through the inertia of no by seeking new possibilities and finding valuable solutions.

Almost 15 years after Einstein wrote that light is made of particles called quanta, outside experiments proved his assertions to be true. Until then, from the time he suggested it, all physicists said, "No way. That's impossible."

But because he was able to think beyond the prevailing assumptions and consider new possibilities, Einstein broke through the inertia of no.

I realize that starting a discussion of creativity with the example of Einstein may seem pretty intimidating. The lesson you can learn from him, though, isn't really about the theory of relativity. It is about being willing to challenge the assumptions around you. And that's something we can all learn to do.

The Two Components of Creative Thinking

Creativity involves two different thought processes: seeking new possibilities and finding valuable solutions.[2]

SEEKING POSSIBILITIES	FINDING SOLUTIONS
Envisioning	Judging
Imagining	Analyzing
Exploring	Choosing
Originating	Refining
Generating	Critiquing
Diverging	Converging

The biggest mistake
many people make when
it comes to thinking
creatively is moving too
quickly from seeking
possibilities to finding
solutions.

When the inertia of no takes over, it kills off possibility
seeking little by little until we find ourselves out of
balance from a thinking standpoint—fully in critical,
analytical, judgment mode. This can manifest as
irritation, apathy, and dissatisfaction.

INERTIA OF NO VS. CREATIVITY

Whereas the inertia of no leads to sluggish energy,
creativity (a balance of exploring and choosing,
imagining and analyzing) is active and solution-
oriented.

With the inertia of no there is only one path that will benefit some and not others; creativity helps us find win-win solutions. We need it to force us out of the mental state that tends to resist new ideas.

Seeking possibilities and finding solutions is natural for human beings. Thus, when we set out to balance our thinking, we find ourselves in a more natural state of being.

And now I'm going to give you one of my most important series of tips to help you deliberately power-up your own creative thinking.

How to Jumpstart Your Creativity

There's a reason why many writers embrace the 'messy first draft' concept. They lower their expectations on form, exact wording, and even grammar to allow for the flow of ideas. Then they go back to cut, add, and improve the draft.

This is an example of how you can separate possibility seeking and solution finding in daily work. It's a simple tweak that will help you produce original ideas more consistently.

HOW TO HARNESS YOUR CREATIVE THINKING

When you are seeking possibilities, stay in an exploratory, imaginative mindset. Allow wild ideas to emerge without judgment. You will get to evaluate and make judgments later, when it's time to find solutions.

To grow and sustain creativity, it's essential to engage in both types of thinking, but not at the same time.

Tip 1 HOW TO USE GUIDELINES TO SEEK POSSIBILITIES

In his seminal book *Applied Imagination*, Alex Osborn (the "O" founder of BBDO advertising agency) introduced several guiding principles for effective possibility-generating sessions. Here they are, slightly adapted:

1. **Pause judgment.** Wait until later to analyze, choose, and critique.

2. **Let loose.** Think up wild, crazy, and unrealistic ideas.

3. **Share.** Suggest ideas that build on others, or combine two ideas into a new one.

4. **Go big.** The more ideas the better!

These guidelines serve as guardrails that help individuals and groups fend off the pull of anti-creativity and instead step into a mindset that supports successful idea-generation sessions.[3]

Tip 2 SHIFT YOUR PERSPECTIVE

Where are you when your best ideas come to you?

How might you recreate that mindset as you set out on an exploratory mission to seek possibilities? Here are some ideas:

→ Watch a funny video

→ Take a walk in nature

→ Get up from your chair and out of your office into a different setting

→ Read a poem

→ Play ping-pong

→ Tell a joke

→ Power down your screens

→ Spot scenes in the clouds

→ Doodle

→ Blast your favorite song and dance

Tip 3 **TAKE A BREAK**

After you've generated a bunch of ideas, it's ideal to take a break. Stop actively thinking about the topic.

If you're working on a flagship product or developing a new startup business idea, this break might be weeks or months. But, if you're on a tight timeline, maybe it's just a walk to the break room or putting it aside until tomorrow.

In this space between seeking possibilities and critiquing and choosing them, your mind continues to seek possibilities. Often giving yourself that little break will help new ideas and perspectives to emerge.

Tip 4 **HONE YOUR IDEAS**

How do we deal with a wall full of half-baked ideas jotted on Post-it Notes, especially those that go against the norm or seem ridiculous at first glance?

After we've captured all of our ideas, crazy and otherwise, we can use the following guidelines to help us choose ideas better.

1. **Take time.** Give ideas a chance.

2. **Yes, and...** Build on the potential idea to craft an even better one.

3. **Go for wow!** Does the idea excite you? Does it scare you just a little? Is it new and different?

4. **Consult objectives.** Compare ideas to your goals and constraints. Are you on track?

VISIT ONLINE RESOURCES FOR:

Printable postcards to share with your colleagues!

1.5 Case Study: Creativity at the Hardware Store

A few months ago, my friend Erick was frustrated by an annoying problem at home. Every time someone sat on the new chair in his living room, it slipped across the floor. But typical furniture pads didn't work in this case.

So, he went where every good problem solver goes to seek new ideas: to the hardware store.

SEEKING NEW POSSIBILITIES

Erick spent almost an hour walking through the aisles, exploring materials, and imagining possible solutions. He picked up items that might solve his problem and collected them in his cart. During this time he was solely dedicated to seeking new possibilities.

This exploratory thinking propelled his thoughts beyond what presently existed and allowed him to consider what might be possible. Yet, if he only used this type of thinking, it wouldn't be entirely creative. His final result would be a shopping cart full of random materials and his chair would still be slipping across the room. Creativity requires another step.

FINDING VALUABLE SOLUTIONS

After exploring and collecting to his satisfaction, Erick looked through the materials he had gathered, considered his original objectives, and narrowed his options to find a valuable solution.

Though designed for a totally different use, a rubber grommet seemed like it would do the trick.
Four of these set him back about $3.17. He tested them out on the chair, and they worked like a charm.

THE LESSON: EXPLORE AT A STORE

When you need to spark new thinking, visit a retail store or destination stocked with potential solutions. Then imagine alternate uses for the items you see. Allow yourself to make strange and surprising connections. They just may lead to a new idea that solves a problem, or surprises and delights you.

The Two Big Myths about Creativity

In this book I will directly address and debunk two prevailing myths I often hear about creativity:

Myth 1 **CREATIVITY IS ABOUT THE ARTS**

Creativity is the robust thinking that allows us to imagine and open up new opportunities and solutions. It *includes* making art, music, and poetry but it goes far beyond these disciplines. Creativity is also about solving problems and can be applied to business, science, government, and just about every other sector.

Myth 2 **SOME PEOPLE AREN'T CREATIVE AT ALL**

This is false. You might not have thought that my friend's trip to the hardware store or the fabulous meal you made by throwing together surprising ingredients from your pantry are creative acts, but they are—we all have the capacity to accomplish them every day.

 1.7 **Take a Page from Art School**

One reason we associate creativity with art is because the arts do creativity well. People who attend art schools are trained to think in ways that support productive creativity across domains.

In many cases, this means professors encourage students to spend a significant amount of time proposing unique approaches to their work.

For example, a common art school assignment is to create sometimes as many as 100 quick concept sketches. Just think of having to come up with 100 ideas before you even get to begin your project. What's the point?

Theoretically, the initial ideas that pop into your head are going to be the most obvious and least original.

As you work, you gain momentum that propels you to think in completely different ways so you don't repeat yourself. You begin to play with ideas and make surprising combinations. You might get tired along the way and include ideas with little value, but they lead to others. Then you're at 95 and you have 5 more to go. You simply can't think of one more thing, so you take a break. During your break you get a few more and suddenly you're at 100.

In this way, students invest time to seek possibilities as a first step to tackle a project. This is not unlike a basketball player practicing free throws. You're building a skill and increasing the chance that you're going to get a good shot.

Art students slowly learn that when they force themselves to suggest lots of ideas, they push beyond the obvious to reach truly original ideas.

Only after they complete the sketches, and usually on a different day, are they asked to find solutions. They factor in the objectives of the assignment, the grading rubric, and skills they want to develop to choose the concept that best fits.

This process is supported by an underlying openness that actively welcomes new ideas.

Using an approach like this, art school students are encouraged to stretch outside their comfort zones.

Most importantly, they are encouraged to throw ideas out there without knowing whether or not they will work.

LIST EVERYTHING THAT MAKES YOU SMILE

Working with a group in a fun and game-like facilitated ideation session is one thing, but on your own it would be impossible to come up with 100 ideas for a project, right?

I believe that you can do it, especially if you start out with something you know well: yourself. Get a little notebook or open a new note on your phone. Write at the top, "What are all the things that make me smile?"

As you make your list, number it so you know when you get to 100. Work on it in one sitting if you'd like, or stretch it out over the day or the week. The point is to get to 100 and observe your process as you do it. Is there any point when you notice yourself approaching the list differently?

Nine Things Creative People Never Say

When a star dies, scientists believe all that's left is a black hole that sucks up anything that crosses its path. The same thing can happen in an environment that lacks creativity.

When we and those around us fail to exercise our creative thinking consistently, our creativity also seems to die.

The inertia of no turns CREATIVE into REACTIVE.

The inertia of no is the absence of active creativity.

Because it can only deal with what already exists and never makes anything new, the inertia of no creates either a harshly judgmental, reactionary mentality or an atmosphere where people really don't care.

→ "It's impossible."

→ "If we try something new it might not work."

→ "That's not how we do things around here."

→ "This is what we should do."

→ "Let's go with this idea because it's our only one."

→ "There's no solution."

→ "It's never worked so I'm not even going to try."

→ "We're stuck."

→ "It doesn't follow our normal procedures."

Unfortunately, many of us have experienced the slow death of our creativity.

> **Story:** **PROOF THAT YOU WERE BORN CREATIVE**
>
> In 1968, George Land gave 1,600 four- and five-year-old children a creativity test he had developed to find innovators for engineering and design positions at NASA. This test specifically measured a person's seeking possibility skills.
>
> He tested the same children again when they were 10 and again at age 15. Land and his team compared these scores with a large sample of adults who also took the assessment.
>
> Here's what he found: Only 2% of adults scored in the creative genius range compared to 98% of five-year-olds. This was an astounding revelation.
>
> Yet Land remained optimistic by looking at the data in the opposite way: 98% of five-year-olds scored the same as NASA creative geniuses.
>
> Everyone has the innate capacity to be creative.
>
> Land concluded, "What we have seen in our work with adults is that the five-year-old creative genius is still lurking inside—just waiting to break free."[4]
>
> No matter who you are, creativity can be re-awakened and trained back into action.

Creativity is Shifting Your Thinking

Due to inertia, a tennis ball will not move unless an outside force is exerted on it.

Thinking is the same way. Our thoughts tend to gravitate toward sameness, toward thinking what we already think. They are bounded by our own assumptions, biases, and perceived limitations. This is the inertia of no.

Creativity is about shifting our thinking. To grow our creativity, we have to be deliberate about sparking this shift to consistently keep our thoughts moving toward possibility.

The fundamental challenge is being willing to break through the inertia of no. We all have the power to do this, and the next chapter shows why it's a matter of survival that we do.

CHAPTER SUMMARY:
THREE THINGS TO REMEMBER

→ Creativity is breaking through the inertia of no by seeking new possibilities and finding valuable solutions.

→ Creative thinking involves two overarching thought processes: envisioning/imagining/exploring and judging/analyzing/choosing. It's critical that these each get their own time and place.

→ When we stretch ourselves to come up with a greater quantity of ideas, they are more likely to be truly original.

CHAPTER 2

Why Creativity Matters

In our changing world, the costs of not using creativity are higher than ever.

We can become stagnant in our jobs by when we run out of ways to add value. We might become so enamored with prior successes that we get blindsided by new competitors. We might become paralyzed by the unfamiliar and retreat into the temporary comfort of what we've always done.

What Happens If You Don't Get Creative?

"The practical reality is that any present-tense version of the world is unstable. What we currently consider to be true—both objectively and subjectively—is habitually provisional."

— Chuck Klosterman, But What If We're Wrong?

Today's mantra is, "If you don't want to get disruptED, become the disruptOR."

This applies to individuals, whether employees or entrepreneurs, just as it applies to teams and entire companies.

When many jobs are on the verge of becoming extinct due to automation, outsourcing, or new inventions, it is creativity that allows us to think up ways to go forward rather than wait to get downsized and bemoan our fate. It is creativity that helps us to see patterns amidst the change and invent new roles for ourselves.

On the flip side of all the disruption, there is tremendous opportunity for those who are willing to use their creativity to adapt to change.

2.2 Change at the Speed of... Nuclear Shock Waves

In many cases, disrupted companies like Blockbuster or Sears simply did not know what hit them. They did not anticipate the speed and scope of change.

In his book *The Inevitable,* founder of *Wired Magazine* and futurist Kevin Kelly proposed that information is growing at almost the same velocity as a nuclear shock wave, or 6,000 square meters of information storage material per second![1]

Consider another metric: the number of US patents that are granted every year. Except for a blip during World War II, the number of patents issued has mirrored the exponential growth curve. Right now, we are living on the steep, accelerating part of the curve.

Patents signify new inventions which become products that get incorporated into our lives. This is just one dimension of the change in which we live.[2]

Story: **4 STEPS TO SELL A FOOTBALL TEAM**

Matt Hall, head of upper campus at Rippowam Cisqua School just outside of New York City, is experienced in leading organizations through dramatic change.

In a prior job, it was Hall's responsibility to start a football program at a school that had long prided itself in not having a football program.

But by the end of his tenure, the new football program's most vocal critic had become its most ardent supporter.

Here's how he did it:

Step 1 **UNDERSTAND THAT CHANGE IS REALITY**

Hall started every presentation about the new football initiative with a conversation about change.

Step 2 **NAME WHAT WILL STAY THE SAME**

At the same time, Hall assured people that many other things would stay the same. He pointed out specifics.

Step 3 **IDENTIFY YOUR COMFORT LEVEL**

Hall then showed his Comfort with Change Spectrum (next section) and asked people to identify where they presently stood, in general and with regard to the new program.

Step 4 **MOVE ALONG THE CONTINUUM**

Hall's strategy and talking points helped people in his community move along the continuum to embrace the new program.

The Comfort with Change Spectrum

2.3

Active Resister | In Denial | Need a Nudge | Open Arms

Which category best describes how you feel about change?

Active Resister

The active resister category is represented by a bottle of poison. That's how you feel about change.

In Denial

You'd rather turn the page and keep doing what you are doing because it's going just fine right now, thank you very much.

Need a Nudge

You may not have thought too much about change before, but reading these chapters helps you consider how it relates to you.

Open Arms

Yes, yes, yes! This is so exciting. You are ready for the next iteration!

Three Tips To Help You Embrace Change

Tip 1 **PRETEND IT'S OPPOSITE DAY**

Try doing the opposite of what you normally do. If you usually wear gray and black, go bright. If you walk, run. If you go to the gym, take a walk. Read a book instead of scrolling on your phone. Shake things up just a little bit to crack open the door to change.

Tip 2 **MOVE YOUR FURNITURE**

A great way to shift your perspective is to try shifting your own surroundings to move the needle on your change tolerance.

Slide your computer monitor to the opposite end of your desk. Turn the table the other way. Switch your wall hangings. Go wild and draw on your sparkling clean whiteboard.

Tip 3 **LEARN TO PIVOT**

Jenny Blake, a former career development specialist at Google, is an author and podcaster extraordinaire. Her motto is, "If change is the only constant, let's get better at it." To that end, Blake wrote the book *Pivot: The Only Move That Matters Is Your Next One* to help people learn to take the small steps needed to constantly shift with change and keep moving forward in their careers.

2.5 Learn Constantly, Like Great-Grandma

I like to imagine how my husband's great-grandmother, Nam-Nam, would have reacted to a full throttle ride in a Tesla. After all, when she was young she rode in one of the original electric cars that could reach a whopping 14 miles per hour.

The change that Nam experienced in her lifetime was astounding. When she was born in 1901, the world was still in slow acceleration mode. But toward the end of her life, in the early 2000s, growth was (and it still is) like rapid acceleration in a Tesla. It's almost ludicrous! Yet, even at age 100, Nam was up on the news and taking computer lessons. Nam-Nam's secret? She was always willing to learn something new.

NAM-NAM'S PRINCIPLES FOR THRIVING WITH CHANGE

Principle 1 **ASK, ASK, ASK**

Nam was curious and she wasn't afraid to ask. If there is something you don't know, just ask. And don't just ask Siri. Ask a real person like Nam would have done.

Principle 2 **ALWAYS BE LEARNING**

What have you learned lately? What do you want to learn tomorrow?

Principle 3 **KNOW HOW YOU LIKE TO LEARN**

In what ways do you learn most effectively?

Do you learn best when you:

→ Listen?

→ See visuals like charts and maps?

→ Read?

→ Use metaphors and analogies?

→ Make a tangible product?

→ Teach?

→ Discuss with others?

→ Pair ideas with music?

→ Move around?

→ Write?

→ Doodle?

When you know how you learn best, you can incorporate these techniques more often and maximize your motivation for continuous learning.

2.6 Case Study: How Old Ideas Can Be Creative

By the 1980s, Yellowstone was in trouble. An overpopulation of elk had decimated its trees, plants, and grass. New thinking was needed to figure out a way to reverse the decay in the ecosystem.

The resulting "new" idea was to bring back the wolves who had been earlier eliminated from the park and who find elk delicious.

Within years, trees shot up and vegetation regenerated. Birds came back in abundance, along with beavers, rabbits, and mice. The tree growth diminished erosion and even the geography of the rivers changed for the better.[3]

Naturalists didn't clone a new species to solve the problem and they didn't douse the park with pesticides to spur plant growth. They actually returned the ecosystem to its original state.

But because they reversed "the way things had been done for a long time"—which involved dispelling a long-held fear of wolves—their solution can be a considered new, valuable, and therefore creative.

Story: **SHINOLA CREATES ARTISANAL WATCHES**

Shinola has developed its own "artisanal" approach to manufacturing watches, leather goods, and even bicycles.

The company combines the latest technology with high-touch, personalized product assembly. Their watchmakers receive Swiss training and 30 people are involved in assembling a single watch.

Watchmaking as a trade has been around for centuries but for the most part, factories have taken over the job. By bringing back the "master craftsman" approach, Shinola created a new twist on an old idea and a compelling story that endears customers to its brand.[4]

VISIT ONLINE RESOURCES FOR:

A video of the Shinola factory tour.

CHAPTER SUMMARY: THREE THINGS TO REMEMBER

→ Creativity helps us avoid getting disrupted and instead become the disruptor.

→ Creative thinking can lead to "old" ideas applied under new circumstances.

→ If you're not comfortable with change, work on increasing your change tolerance.

CHAPTER 3

Are You Creative?

For over 20 years, I have been writing, speaking, and teaching clients of all ages how to discover and apply their creativity skills so they can learn and work better. I've learned from the top minds in the fields of creativity, innovation, and education. Now I partner with these same experts to run innovation strategy workshops and professional development trainings at organizations of all sizes.

This work has formalized my knowledge of proven frameworks, research, and practices that guide a pragmatic approach to developing individual, team, and organizational creativity.

In the science of creativity, it's essential to start with the right question.

Asking oneself, *Am I creative?* is not the right question.

In my book *Creativity for Everybody,* written with designer Jane Harvey, we suggest asking this question instead:

VISIT ONLINE RESOURCES FOR:

An exclusive excerpt from *Creativity For Everybody.*

In what ways are you creative?[1]

3.1 How to Get Started with Creative Thinking

I like to picture a flourishing prairie when I think about developing creativity. The prairie is the natural state of the North American plains and it teems with life.

On the prairie, an astounding number of species—from textured grasses and purple wildflowers, to spiders and sparrows--form a diverse web of interactions that make a resilient whole. To withstand tornadoes and heavy flooding, the prairie relies on the unique adaptations of each species working together.

The prairie's resilience is based on the strengths of each individual species.

So is the resilience of our communities, our organizations, our families, and our world.

The compass plant is a poignant example of how important it is to consider individual strengths. If we were to compare it to other flowering prairie plants during their first years of growth, we'd be disappointed.

It can take two to five years for the compass plant to produce its brilliant yellow flowers, initially appearing stunted (or even like a weed).

Photos 1 & 2 Prairie Moon Nursery. Used with Permission.

We have to look below the surface to understand its unique growth trajectory. Before it blooms above ground, the compass plant develops thick roots up to fifteen feet deep.

These roots grow to nourish the soil and help the entire prairie withstand harsh weather conditions.

The compass plant can only strengthen the ecosystem when it proceeds with its own growth.

VISIT ONLINE RESOURCES FOR:

Stunning compass plant photos from National Geographic.

It's the same for us.

When we set out to be more creative, we start by pinpointing and nourishing our own creative strengths. Like the compass plant, sometimes we need to look below the surface to find those strengths.

In the first place, most people don't know what their creative strengths are. Thus, it's likely that these have been underutilized and may have even atrophied into annoying behaviors (see Chapter 7.1). When we identify them and learn to use them, they spur the individual growth that can immediately benefit our ecosystems, too.

 ## Assess Your Creative Strengths

"Solitude can be a catalyst to innovation."

- Susan Cain, Quiet

Often in talks and workshops I share a list of creative strengths, or personal characteristics that support creativity—like being independent, high energy, open-minded, and thorough. I ask participants to pick three that describe them best.

I've done this exercise with thousands of people and no one has ever said, "None apply to me." People love the creative strengths and easily identify with several.

Those who haven't typically considered themselves creative realize they do indeed have creative strengths. They might select empathic or perceptive or thorough, instead of imaginative or original.

These strengths help us see that there is a diverse spectrum of attributes that support creative thought and it expands our view of creativity.

One of the creative strengths that I include is "need alone time." Though creativity is often collaborative, alone time is essential to digging deep and producing original work. It is essential for creativity, though some need it more than others.

I've been surprised over the years to see how many people choose "alone time" as a top strength. Perhaps we're all just overly stressed out and want to chill Or, it shows that people know how important alone time is to realizing their best work.

**DOWNLOAD:
RESOURCE**

Access the Sparkitivity Creative Strengths
Spotter Workbook at www.sparkitivity.com/
strengthsspotter

Creative strengths are internal forces that push us out of the inertia of no and toward possibility.

Here in this book I'd like to give you a new way to look
at your creative strengths: through the lens of how you
like to think. Our preferred ways of thinking point us
to our strengths. If we like doing something, we are
more motivated to do it, which will develop the skill as
a strength. To find your creative thinking strengths, go
to the online resources section now and download the
survey on the next page to help you assess how you
think.

In What Ways Do You Like to Think?

*Spark*itivity

Select all of the following statements that resonate with you:

____ I like to come up with many ideas and a variety of ideas.

____ I often go beyond the obvious to consider the unique and unexpected.

____ When an idea is presented, I like expanding on it and taking it further.

____ I like to simplify, clarify, and get to the essence of a problem.

____ I don't like to rush to close down a problem or project too quickly without depth of thought.

____ I like to use intuition and empathy to understand how someone else might be thinking.

____ I enjoy taking ideas and building scenarios to give them meaning in the real world.

____ I like to make cross connections among unrelated ideas and situations.

____ I need to get visual about concepts, ideas, and processes in order to understand a problem and communicate ideas.

____ I enjoy going beyond the concrete to imagine new possibilities.

____ I value learning and working using multiple senses—movement, sound, taste, touch, smell.

____ I often take a new perspective on something to see things from a different angle.

____ I pay attention to what is behind the scenes or what is not clearly revealed or expressed.

____ I like to rethink barriers and assumptions that we might not be aware of.

____ I value and appreciate a sense of humor when working with others.

____ I like to think into the future, imagining change and possibilities beyond the here and now.

DOWNLOAD: TEMPLATE

"In What Ways Do You Like to Think?" Survey

3.3 How Your Strengths Help You Seek Possibilities

Did you finish the survey? I imagine that if Andy Dunn, CEO and co-founder of clothing brand Bonobos, took this survey, the following thinking preferences would be included in his selections:

→ I like to make cross connections among unrelated ideas and situations.

→ I value and appreciate a sense of humor when working with others.

When Dunn decided to call Bonobos customer service reps "customer experience ninjas," he was connecting two unrelated ideas. When he hired comedians who needed a day job to staff the ninja jobs, he was appreciating the role humor can play when customers call for help.

Each of the ways of thinking listed on the survey supports us in our endeavor to seek new possibilities, like Dunn did. They represent the varied dimensions of divergent thinking, the type of thinking George Land measured in his study of the creative genius of children and adults.

"Divergent thinking" is the technical term for seeking new possibilities.

Divergent thinking helps us generate many new ideas, imagine, be original, ask questions, spot problems, look for patterns, make unexpected connections, and see things from a variety of perspectives.

When we know which ways we prefer to think divergently, we can deliberately call upon them when we are faced with a challenge or need to shift our thinking.

Divergent thinking strengths help us do the rigorous gymnastics of the mind that lead us to unexpected solutions.

For example, let's say you selected this survey question as a top preference:

I enjoy taking ideas and building scenarios to give them meaning in the real world.

This means that you like to make things tangible and concrete, to put them into context.

BUILD A MODEL OF AN ABSTRACT CONCEPT

I like to run an activity in workshops that draws on the above strength. Each team gets a box of materials and I present a challenge related to the topic at hand. At times, the challenge has been, "Build a model that illustrates your team's definition of creativity." As they work with the materials, teams tinker, discuss, and ultimately share incredibly insightful learnings gleaned during the process.

Recall that my definition of creativity includes both seeking new possibilities (divergent thinking) and finding valuable solutions (convergent thinking).

Most of us need to build our possibility-seeking skills.

Divergent thinking propels our thoughts beyond what presently exists and allows us to consider what might be possible.

"Creativity is the highest form of mental functioning."

- E. Paul Torrance

Story: **WHERE DID THESE THINKING STRENGTHS COME FROM?**

Back in the middle of the 20th century, IQ had a stranglehold on society's predominant concept of intelligence. It was generally understood that high IQ equaled high intelligence.

Yet, psychologists had been gradually recognizing the importance of a type of thinking not measured by IQ tests— creativity. To prove creative thinking's value as a component of intelligence, they had to identify it as a separate cognitive function.

E. Paul Torrance, often called the "Father of Creativity," spent decades studying creativity empirically. The sixteen thinking preference statements listed on the survey are derived from his work identifying central cognitive skills that underlie creative thinking; each one references a slightly different thought process and each is a thinking strength.[2]

How to Make Strengths Productive at Work

You've already accomplished three things toward making your strengths productive:

1. **Aware of Creativity:** If you marked even one of the statements on the survey, you know that you already think creatively and don't mind doing it.

2. **Identify Strengths:** To use your strengths, you need to know what they are.

3. **Gain Self-Knowledge:** You have made observations about how you think. When you know more about your own thinking processes, you improve your metacognition.

> *"Metacognition allows us to maximize the horsepower of our minds."*
>
> *- Puccio, Mance, and Murdock[3]*

HOW TO MAKE STRENGTHS PRODUCTIVE

1. **Identify.** Write down one of your favorite ways to think, from the survey.

2. **Present uses.** Write the ways you use it now.

3. **Brainstorm a list.** What might be all the ways I can use this strength at work?

4. **Choose.** Select one idea from your list to deliberately employ the creative thinking strength.

CHAPTER SUMMARY:
THREE THINGS TO REMEMBER

→ Instead of "Am I creative?" ask, "In what ways am I creative?"

→ Simply being aware of one's creative strengths goes a long way toward improving creativity.

→ You can deliberately employ your creative strengths and preferences to help you come up with new and different ideas.

CHAPTER 4

How to Gain Creative Confidence

Kristen Bennie has worked at the intersection of design and technology for over two decades. In her current role, she created and developed Open Experience (OX)—collaborative innovation spaces and strategies at Royal Bank of Scotland, both at its headquarters in Edinburgh and in Shoreditch, London. Bennie is responsible for leading the team charged with creating the next generation of innovative products and services at the bank.

At OX, Bennie has trained thousands of bank employees and customers to be more creative in their jobs, using principles like those in this book. She has found a pattern.

Most people know creativity is important, but they don't know how to get started. At the core of it, they lack confidence in seeking possibilities.

Yet, after Bennie's trainings, most embrace a new way of working based on creative thinking principles. When they go back to their day jobs or departments, this starts to shift their teams toward possibility.

Most people's initial trepidations relate to misconceptions about what creativity is in the first place. When we are aware that creativity is a combination of seeking possibilities and finding solutions—and that we already use these modes of thinking—we gain comfort and can work to do it more deliberately.

Kristen Bennie's Tip **THE POWER OF OBSERVATION**

Taking the time to observe and truly see the world around us is inspirational and full of wonderful possibilities. Try being a "fly on the wall" for an hour or an afternoon. Pick an environment that you don't normally spend time in and observe. Make it your business to simply be part of that environment and work on your observation skills. What's happening? How do people interact? What surprises you? Use the AEIOU technique to frame your observation, focusing on:

→ **A**CTIVITIES

→ **E**NVIRONMENTS

→ **I**NTERACTIONS

→ **O**BJECTS

→ **U**SERS

To validate your insights, try this exercise in multiple locations and environments to understand what is the same and what is different.

Three Tips to Practice Your Creativity

Have you ever jumped off a cliff? Unlikely, if you're reading this book (unless you enjoy cliff dive swimming, of course). Have you ever jumped off a very high platform while safely harnessed to a zipline? If you want to experience the exhilaration of jumping off of something tall, but you don't want to die, a zipline is usually a much better way to go than a cliff.

Guidelines, tools, and processes are like a zipline for creativity.

They provide safe scaffolding as we work within a structure that, if done well, helps us harness our creativity and drive toward new possibilities.

Tip 1 **RESPOND LIKE AN IMPROV ACTOR**

Imagine if, in the middle of an improv scene, one actor told the other, "You weren't supposed to say that!" or "Don't use that line!" The improv actor's secret success tool is staying in a mentality of "Yes, and . . ." She has to say yes to the ridiculous and go with it to finish out the scene well. Today, practice responding to people's ideas with, "Yes, and . . . " Repeat tomorrow.

Tip 2 **THINK LIKE A POET**

Poets are known for being keen observers of life and nature. They are also known for keeping a little notebook on them at all times to jot down random thoughts. Get yourself a tiny notebook and keep it with you for one week. At least once a day, sit where you don't usually sit, like on your office sofa or your back porch. Jot down ten things that you notice. Peruse your notebook often, especially when you're stuck on a problem or need a new idea.

Tip 3 **DO IT DIFFERENTLY**

It is the inertia of no that pulls us to look around at others to inform what we do, what we buy, and even how we speak. This conformity pull has become more acute with social media, where we can peek in on our neighbors 24/7/365.

Today, notice seven things that you do because other people do them. Recall this book's introduction about my shoes, for example. Write them down. Then, make a commitment to change one that will improve your life. Do it differently. Take a risk.

4.2 How to Tame Your Inner Critic

Editing means correcting, choosing, condensing. These are all aspects of judgment and analytical thinking, useful when developing solutions but barriers to seeking possibilities.

Most of us have taken on this framework and constantly edit ourselves and our thoughts. This is what Jim Friedman, professor of creativity and entrepreneurship at the Miami University Farmer School of Business, calls the 'voice of judgment.' Others have termed it the 'inner critic' or the 'negative news network.'

Friedman has found that the voice of judgment is a core block to creativity: "It's the inner doubt, that voice that says, 'You're not good enough. Somebody else thought of this. Somebody else is more creative than you are." He devotes an entire class session to the topic and assigns students a significant project to help them address their own self-criticism that runs alongside intense sensitivity to peer judgment.

Being aware of your own voice of judgment is important to gaining the metacognition needed to improve your creativity.

Awareness helps you spot your inner critic when it tries to stop you from putting forth a new idea or taking a risk as you seek possibilities. You can even learn to harness it pragmatically during solution finding when you're analyzing and improving ideas.

 ## 4.3 How to Beat Imposter Syndrome

"The counterfeit innovator is wildly self-confident. The real one is scared to death."

- Steven Pressfield, The War of Art

Who cares if you're not Monet?

Sometimes people wield harsh judgments upon themselves because they feel their creativity is inadequate.

They don't think they are creative because they compare themselves to others who are famously creative, like Miles Davis or Maya Angelou. Yet Maya Angelou herself struggled with the very same thoughts!

> *"I have written 11 books, but each time I think 'Uh-oh, they're going to find out now. I've run a game on everybody, and they're going to find me out.'"*
>
> —*Maya Angelou*

This feeling that one is a fake or a fraud has been termed imposter syndrome. Most of us struggle with it at one time or another; a recent study put that number at 70% of professionals surveyed.[1]

When we're dealing with the distinctly personal act of voicing new ideas to the world, imposter syndrome tends to rear its ugly head of self-doubt.

Whenever it starts whispering to you that you're not good enough to be creative, or that you're a fake, remember that it's just another form of anti-creativity— the inertia of no masquerading as your own thoughts.

Go forward anyway. Turn self-doubt into motivation that fuels your best work. And read this gallery of quotes from famous creators past and present to remember you're not alone.

GALLERY OF QUOTES: FAMOUS CREATORS FEEL LIKE FAKE CREATIVES, TOO[2]

> *"No matter what we've done, there comes a point where you think, 'How did I get here? When are they going to discover that I am, in fact, a fraud and take everything away from me?'"*
>
> - Tom Hanks

"I still sometimes feel like a loser kid in high school and I just have to pick myself up and tell myself that I'm a superstar every morning so that I can get through this day and be for my fans what they need for me to be."

- Lady Gaga

"I am not a writer. I've been fooling myself and other people."

- John Steinbeck

"Every time I'm making a movie . . . I have the same fear that I'm gonna be fired. And I'm not joking. Every movie, the first week, I always feel that they could fire me."

-Penélope Cruz

"Ah, the impostor syndrome!? The beauty of the impostor syndrome is you vacillate between extreme egomania, and a complete feeling of: 'I'm a fraud! Oh god, they're on to me! I'm a fraud!' So you just try to ride the egomania when it comes and enjoy it, and then slide through the idea of fraud. Seriously, I've just realized that almost everyone is a fraud, so I try not to feel too bad about it."

- Tina Fey

CHAPTER SUMMARY:
THREE THINGS TO REMEMBER

→ When your inner critic tries to persuade you to avoid taking a risk, use it as motivation to move forward anyway.

→ Creativity tools and principles help us practice safe risks and grow creatively.

→ If you ever feel like a creative fraud, look to the most famous creators of all time to commiserate and then overcome it and move on.

CHAPTER 5

How to Overcome the Barriers to Creativity

If you were watching comedies in the early 1990s (or if you enjoy cult classics) the word *change* might conjure up the *Wayne's World* scene where Rob Lowe asks Dana Carvey how he'd feel about making a change.

"We fear change," Carvey responds, expressionless, as he proceeds to systematically bash a slowly moving robotic arm with a hammer.

VISIT ONLINE RESOURCES FOR:

A link to watch the full video scene from Wayne's World.

Maybe this is a "you had to be there" moment, in the room when my high school friends and I saw the movie, but Carvey's character was on point. Mostly, we do fear change. To overcome the blocks to creativity, it's important to face them head-on.

5.1 Every Barrier to Creativity Starts with One Emotion

Fear is the stubborn core of the inertia of no that blocks creative thinking. Rick Pollak, director of people analytics at PwC, has helped employees overcome specific fears across several top companies where he's worked.

Have you wrestled with any of the following?

→ Fear of making a mistake

→ Fear of standing out

→ Fear of degrading a relationship

→ Fear of causing a process to malfunction

→ Fear of not having enough time

→ Fear of losing your job

→ _____ [add your own]

These fears rear up in little ways all day long, every day, mostly in the form of our own thoughts whispering to us like a little "devil of no" on our shoulders.

5.2 Why Getting Rejected Is a Good Thing

A guy named Jia Jiang walks into PetSmart and asks for a haircut.

"For what kind of dog?" inquires the woman at the counter.

"How much would it cost to trim *my* hair?" asks Jiang.

The conversation that ensues is entertaining and the PetSmart clerk has a great sense of humor about it. Jiang even promises to refrain from barking. But, ultimately, he is rejected.

They only trim animals at PetSmart, not people.

This is just one instance in Jia Jiang's 100 Days of Rejection personal challenge.

VISIT ONLINE RESOURCES FOR:

A link to watch Jia Jiang get rejected at PetSmart.

"People who really changed the world, who changed the way we live and the way we think, are the people who were met by initial and often violent rejection... People like Martin Luther King, Jr., Nelson Mandela, and even Jesus Christ... They did not let rejection define them."

- Jia Jiang[1]

Fear of rejection is a significant mental barrier that prevents us from taking the risk to think or act creatively.

Jiang had realized that his fear of rejection was crippling him from pursuing his dreams. He set out on a personal challenge to become more comfortable going out on a limb, based on the Rejection Therapy game created by Canadian entrepreneur Jason Comely—you win if you get rejected by another person.

Through this exercise, Jiang became more resilient, landed his dream teaching job, and became a famous YouTuber. He also learned one more secret that I'll share in the next section.

MISTAKES + CREATIVE THINKING = AWESOME INVENTIONS

Don't you think the ice cream vendor who ran out of serving dishes at the sweltering 1904 World's Fair was kicking himself? He was, until the nearby Persian waffle maker rolled up one of his waffles, put a scoop of ice cream on top, and the ice cream cone was born.

You can read compelling stories like this one in my favorite book of all time to help convince adults and kids alike to stop letting "perfect be the enemy of trying": *Mistakes that Worked: The World's Familiar Inventions and How They Came to Be,* by Charlotte Foltz Jones and John O'Brien.

"Your biggest failure is the thing you dreamed of contributing but didn't find the guts to do."

- Seth Godin, *The Icarus Deception*

Story:	**PEOPLE MIGHT SURPRISE YOU**

This year, I participated in Jia Jiang's seven-day rejection challenge. For each of seven consecutive days, I had to ask a stranger to take a selfie with me. The first day I gave the excuse that I was doing a challenge. The stranger agreed, but it was sort of odd because I didn't know the three primary principles:

Principle 1: Ask with joy and confidence.

Principle 2: Provide a genuine reason for your ask.

Principle 3: Your reason can't be, "I'm doing a rejection therapy challenge."

So the second day I said I was creating an album of selfies with strangers. The guy paused, accepted, and really seemed to enjoy it.

The third day I was much more confident, and my selfie request seemed to make the woman's day.

In rejection therapy, the point isn't to get rejected. It's to push past the fear of getting rejected that prevents us from seeking new possibilities.

People surprise us with their willingness to accommodate even an outlandish request if we're just brave enough to ask.

So why don't you try it?

 ## How to Get Rejected (On Purpose)

Here's how to use the guidelines for creative thinking to help you overcome a fear of failure or discomfort.

Step 1 **GET INTO A FUN AND OPEN MINDSET**

Start by exploring Jia Jiang's 100 Days of Rejection website or download DareMe, the app he created based on Rejection Therapy.

VISIT ONLINE RESOURCES FOR:

A link to 100 Days of Rejection

Step 2 **SEEK POSSIBILITIES**

Recall the seek possibilities guidelines in Chapter 1.4, Tip 1. Now, come up with ten to fifteen ideas on how you might get rejected.

Step 3 **TAKE A QUICK BREAK**

Go to the restroom, get a breath of fresh air, or do something totally different. Your break can be five minutes or five hours. When you put space between seeking possibilities and finding solutions, new ideas emerge. You'll have a different perspective when you start finding solutions.

Step 4 **FIND AN AMAZING SOLUTION**

Recall the finding solutions guidelines in Chapter 1.4, Tip 4. Consider what's most important to you in choosing the way you're going to get rejected. Do you want it to be quick? Right in your neighborhood? Low prep? Generate a potentially hysterical story to tell? Jot down three criteria and filter your ideas through them.

Step 5 **GET REJECTED**

As you set out on this mission, you WILL feel uncomfortable and weird. Expect the discomfort and go with it. Remember, this is all in fun and after it's over you can think back on the experience as a story to tell.

The One Big Question Creative People Ask

Creative people start by replacing *no* with *why.*

Jia Jiang found during his rejection experiment that sometimes people said no to him straightaway. Instead of taking no for the final word, he learned to ask, "Why?" to look for possibilities. As a result, his experience was much richer and he was helpful to people.

PRACTICE WHY

Whether you are a school teacher, civil servant, or board chair, people ask you questions all day long. Try this approach to improve your responses.

Step 1 **OBSERVE QUESTIONS YOU ARE ASKED**

→ Jot down the questions and your responses.

Step 2 **REFLECT ON THE CONVERSATIONS**

→ What is the nature of the questions?

→ Do you often say no?

→ What did you discover?

Step 3 **TOMORROW, TRY TO AVOID NO**

→ Dig deeper into people's motivations by replacing no with why.

Step 4 **REFLECT ON YOUR CONVERSATIONS**

→ What new insights did you have?

→ What new insights did you notice others have?

Example: **IS NO STILL USEFUL?**

No is still a valid response in certain situations. Or is it?

"Can I run into the middle of the highway?" No.

Even when no seems obvious, a why instead usually reveals something more.

"Can I run into the middle of the highway?" Why?

"My drone accidentally flew to the other side." OR

"Can I work from home three days a week?" Why?

"Traffic has gotten worse and it takes me an extra hour and a half to commute per day. I have to leave earlier so I can no longer send early emails to our team in India. It's starting to back up our workflow..."

Now we have a solvable problem. The solution may be that you work from home three days a week. Or, it may be something else. But by resisting no and asking why, we allow for exploration and clarity.

5.5 How to Embrace a Possibility Mindset

Replacing *no* with *why* is the first step in shifting to a possibility mindset. The second is to frame challenges as questions. But not any kind of question will do; they have to be possibility questions.[2]

The way we ask a question can make or break our chance to come up with the new solutions we need.

To open up space for new ideas, we can open up our questions.

Possibility questions are similar to *What if* questions but are more focused on finding solutions.

To frame challenges as questions, all you need to know are two main question starters.

→ How might we...?

→ What might be all the ways...?

These two question starters will help you turn your problems into powerful possibility questions that open up pathways for new thinking and amazing solutions.

VISIT ONLINE RESOURCES FOR:

A link to the video "Making School Better with Just One Question."

HOW TO TURN PROBLEMS INTO POSSIBILITIES

PROBLEM	POSSIBILITY QUESTION
We don't have money for it.	What might be all the ways to get funding?
We are too busy to think creatively.	How might we free up time to dedicate to creative thinking?
Customers might not like it.	How might we prototype ideas so a sampling of customers can try them and give feedback?
Our leadership isn't bold enough to do something innovative.	What might be all the ways to demonstrate the value of this idea to leadership?

WRITE YOUR OWN POSSIBILITY QUESTIONS

Now it's your turn.

Step 1 **IDENTIFY PROBLEMS**

Write down five of the biggest challenges you are working on right now. Or, use the list of things that bother you from Chapter 1.

Step 2 **TURN PROBLEMS INTO POSSIBILITIES**

Use the question starters:

→ How might...?

→ What might be all the ways...?

and the samples on the previous page as a guide to turn each challenge into a possibility question.

Step 3 **CHOOSE ONE TO WORK ON EARNESTLY**

Apply the seeking possibility guidelines to think up new ideas, and the finding solutions guidelines to help you choose and develop the best ones.

Now whenever a seemingly ominous challenge comes your way, you can simply begin with one of the two question starters to turn the block into a possibility question. Evaluate your question by making sure the way it is asked invites new ideas rather than communicates shutdown. Once you get into the habit of doing this, you will have embraced a possibility mindset.

**CHAPTER SUMMARY:
THREE THINGS TO REMEMBER**

→ Fear takes many forms to prevent creative thinking.

→ Deliberately trying to get rejected is a fun way to experience and overcome the discomfort that sometimes hinders creativity.

→ Possibility questions are the creative thinker's superpowers. Every time you ask a question, try starting with *How might we...?* or *What might be all the ways...?*

PART TWO

How To Foster A Creative Environment

CHAPTER 6

How to Create a Possibility Ecosystem

A possibility ecosystem is a context—home, team, entire organization—in which people are aware of, and employ, the mindsets, tools, and processes that support creativity. A possibility ecosystem supports the sustained growth that results in positive change. The result of the products, theories, ideas, or solutions developed within a possibility ecosystem is innovation, or social or personal change.

Possibility ecosystems begin with you.

 ## 6.1 The Three Elements of a Possibility Ecosystem

Whether or not you think of yourself as a creative leader, you can always make your own micro-possibility ecosystems wherever you go. Start by creating one for yourself, then extend it out to others with every interaction you have.

A teacher can create a possibility ecosystem within the classroom. A parent can create a possibility ecosystem within the home. A town rep can create a possibility ecosystem in every meeting with constituents. A consultant can create a possibility ecosystem in the workshops she facilitates.

There are three intertwining elements that create possibility ecosystems. "Yes" responses to the following questions indicate that you're already demonstrating these elements.

Element 1 **HOW YOU VIEW YOURSELF**

→ Do you believe you are capable of thinking creatively?

→ Do you know and use your creative thinking strengths to seek possibilities and find helpful solutions?

Element 2 **HOW YOU VIEW AND INTERACT WITH OTHERS**

→ Do you believe others are capable of thinking creatively?

→ Do you communicate curiosity, ask possibility questions, and give feedback that allows room for original thinking?

Element 3 **HOW YOU SOLVE PROBLEMS**

→ Do you use tools and strategies that unlock the full range of thinking of you and your group?

→ Do you employ deliberate problem-solving processes that support the emergence, development, and implementation of new possibilities?

Possibility ecosystems can be scaled up to a team, a department, or an organization by modeling and teaching creativity mindsets, principles, and practices to others.[1]

When it comes to bringing a possibility ecosystem to life within an organization, the process is typically led by those whom we call change agents. Let's explore what it takes to be a person like that.

 ## How to Be a Change Agent

Most company mission statements include the words *innovation* or *creativity,* but this tends to be wishful thinking because creativity is not usually baked into the way business gets done. It takes change agents to make it actually happen.

INTERNATIONAL BANK CUSTOMER SERVICE TRANSFORMED

The customer service arm of ABN AMRO Services Company (part of the Dutch bank before it was bought by Bank of America) used to be so inadequate that service reps had to undergo special training to handle the continuous flood of irate customers throwing f-bombs.

Even before being an intrapreneur (someone who thinks like an entrepreneur while working inside a corporate environment) was a thing, Elizabeth Hayduk helped transform client feedback from expletives to actual comments that customer service was "da bomb!"

Many of Hayduk's efforts centered around developing employee empathy for the customer experience. She launched a grassroots awareness campaign to help customer service reps see how their actions could positively impact real people, not as cogs in a big impersonal company, but as part of a wider human effort throughout the bank.

Hayduk helped the bank implement a new customer relationship management system so the sales team could capture customer service issues and funnel the data back to operations to help find and fix root causes.

Since her work required changing and investing in systems, another key to her success was having a senior level executive sponsor. She said,

"Equally important to a change agent is a change executive."

When we ask people to be change agents within an organization, leadership support is essential.

 ## How to Find Your Allies

In any industry, it's much easier to be a change agent when you know you have people in your corner who will support you through the ups and downs.

For example, if a school climate is diametrically opposed to new thinking, it is likely that a possibility-focused teacher will become frustrated unless he or she finds allies.

You might wonder, can this work even in a toxic culture resistant to change?

The most honest answer is sometimes. For example, a colleague of mine recently took a job in what you might call an anti-possibility organization.

Even within an unsupportive culture, she is creating her own micro-possibility ecosystem with her clients by tending to each of the three essential elements.

How? She believes she is capable of thinking creatively; uses her creative thinking strengths; interacts with her clients using tools like possibility questions; and employs approaches that support creative thinking like those I will share in Part Three of this book.

You can do this, too.

But the truth is, if the place where you work doesn't support your long-term creative growth, over time you will probably end up finding a new place that does.

For now, find some allies where you are.

 ## Caution! Pay Attention to People on the Edge

". . . we need to head for the edges, the places where we expect to find 'extreme' users who live differently, think differently, and consume differently—a collector who owns 1,400 Barbies, for instance, or a professional car thief."

- Tim Brown, *Change By Design*

If you ever look out on a prairie and see a tree, chances are you're looking at the prairie's edge.

Trees in background on Spinn Prairie's edge, Reynolds, Indiana

On the edges, predictability ends. The conditions are no longer monolithic with grasses and shrubs. Surprising species mingle. Interesting adaptations form.

Depending on your perspective, edges present either problems or opportunities. Mike Fox, a former prairie restoration consultant, says the edges are where the action is. The edges of the prairie fascinate him.

My background working with outlier thinkers has taught me that often those who don't quite fit in can teach us the most about creative thinking. They can be our best allies as we grow.

Who around you thinks differently? Offers unique perspectives? Sits alone in the cafeteria?

Seek them out. Ask them questions. See if you have found an ally.

WALK AROUND THE RIM OF THE PARTY

When I worked at banks, security guards were my allies. Their jobs center around keen observation, which gives them a unique perspective and new ways of looking at things. At cocktail parties, I love to sneak into the kitchen and chat with caterers. They see the event from a different vantage point, again with great insights. If you don't have a job where you spend time on the edge, seek out people who do. If you do have a job where you spend time on the edge, be confident in sharing your unique perspective.

6.5 Four Secrets to Inspire and Motivate Creative Thinkers

Have you ever hired people for their track record of new thinking and fresh ideas, only to find that they didn't produce the results you expected? (Or, have you been in that situation yourself?) Was the person to blame, or did the team or company culture work against new thinking, and therefore squeeze the person out?

This often happens when an organization or team is not functioning as a possibility ecosystem.

> *"Creativity can be either a gift or a curse. If an individual's creative needs are met, they can become exceptional or gifted, but if their needs are not met, the individual will typically cause problems rather than suppress their creative urges."*
>
> *—Kyung Hee Kim*[2]

When I entered the first course toward my masters degree in creativity and change leadership, I was skeptical. After all, I was already an expert in designing and teaching engaging courses to draw out learners' creative thinking; I had done this successfully for years through my business, Sparkitivity.

On the other hand, most courses I'd taken as a student throughout my life had been quite boring. This is one of the reasons I do what I do to improve the process and outcomes of learning.

Would the International Center for Studies in Creativity live up to its good name and keep this skeptical student engaged in learning, or would I have to revert to my back-of-class note writing to provide activity for my thoughts?

The instructional design nerd that I am, I created a spreadsheet detailing the best practices the professors used in teaching the class. The entirety of the course was one of the most engaging I'd ever taken. Creativity principles were deliberately integrated into the course structure, the activities, and the very words that were used, creating a robust possibility ecosystem in which even the most difficult-to-please students could learn deeply and grow.

CREATIVE LEADERSHIP DRIVES ENGAGEMENT

Gallup consistently finds in its State of the Global Workplace survey that only around 15 percent of employees are engaged with their jobs.

On the other hand, a McKinsey survey showed that a whopping 89 percent of employees are satisfied at work when their companies have leaders who are inspirational, supportive, empowering, and focused on development.[3] That's creative leadership in a nutshell.

When we hire people for their creative thinking, their mandate is to bring fresh ideas.

To help them succeed, leaders and teams must provide a baseline of four things:

1. Clear expectations or goals, including the purpose of the task or project.

2. Freedom in how to achieve the goals.

3. First line of defense against naysayers.

4. Openness to understand and support creative strengths. (Turn to the next chapter for more on how to do this!)

**CHAPTER SUMMARY:
THREE THINGS TO REMEMBER**

→ Creativity thrives in possibility ecosystems, when people, processes, and culture work together to support growth.

→ You can create a possibility ecosystem in your individual interactions with others.

→ People who think differently and have unique perspectives are often found around the edges of the party, or the company.

CHAPTER 7

How to Inspire Creativity in Others

 7.1 ## Start by Spotting Thinking Strengths

Once you start recognizing and more deliberately using your own creative thinking strengths, it's easier to spot them in others.

Either have those around you take the *In What Ways Do You Like to Think?* survey themselves, or use your own observations to make some educated guesses.

THE ART OF SEEING STRENGTHS: LOOK FOR WHAT ANNOYS YOU

One way to spot creative strengths is to start with what annoys you. From a young age, our society focuses on remediating "what's wrong" so this should be easy to do.

Oftentimes an annoying behavior is a sign of an underutilized creative strength.

Do you have a team member who constantly interrupts meetings with puns at inappropriate times? In the right context, this humor can be a creative strength.

What if you specifically ask for an element of humor to be included in a marketing campaign you're developing? Or, you might ask the person to begin each meeting with a funny anecdote. Instead of a culture of constant groans, your possibility ecosystem could grow stronger by engaging this strength to open up a valid pathway for its use.

One of the most popular pages in our book *Creativity for Everybody* shows a creative strength coupled with the negative view for which it might be mistaken. I've included a similar chart here, based on the thinking strengths in this book.

Whenever you see an annoying behavior, pause, ponder the underlying thinking strength that would fuel it, and see if you can spot a strength. Bonus points for figuring out how to put this strength to good use, to turn the annoying into the productive.

9 WAYS CREATIVE STRENGTHS CAN SHOW UP AS PROBLEMS	
CREATIVE STRENGTH	**NEGATIVE VIEW**
Lots of ideas	Annoying
Original	Challenges authority
Elaborates	Talks too much
Finds the essence	Asks too many questions
Stays open	Indecisive
Humanizes with empathy	Overly sensitive
Uses humor	Immature/unprofessional
Imaginative	Flighty
Visualizes	Doodler/time-waster

How to Create a Vision That Inspires

In Chapter 5.5 we talked about turning problems into possibility questions, an effective tool for catalyzing new thinking. But it takes more than an excellent question to inspire people. It takes vision. Here are three steps to follow in order to voice a compelling vision:

Step 1 START WITH FIVE LITTLE WORDS TO HELP YOU SEEK YOUR VISION

It would be great if...[1]

Step 2 IGNITE YOUR IMAGINATION AND DREAM A LITTLE

Shift into "seeking possibilities" mode and write down five to ten responses.

What would be great—for your team, for your clients, for a particular upcoming challenge, for your family?

Step 3 CHOOSE THE MOST COMPELLING OPTION THAT MEETS YOUR OBJECTIVES

EXAMPLE: MY VISION FOR THIS GUIDE

Thinking about my vision for this book, here's my quick list:

→ It would be great if more people could find creativity accessible.

→ It would be great if readers come away seeing themselves in a slightly different light.

→ It would be great if people are empowered by simple ideas that lead to consistent new thinking.

→ It would be great if we could have fewer cultures of no.

→ It would be great if every worker in North America used this book as a manual to move toward possibility and growth.

Looking these over, I wanted to choose one that inspired me and has the potential to inspire others. The last one fits the bill.

This is my vision for this book:

It would be great if every worker in North America used this book as a manual to move toward possibility and growth.

What's your vision?

The Real Secret to Sparking New Ideas

"In redefining or rewording a problem for creative attack, we try to find the question which, if answered successfully, would set in motion the second-order, creative changes that would lead to the solution."

—E. Paul Torrance

The first time I entered the offices of IP and technology firm Ivani, five employees (including the CEO) were huddled together, smiling and balancing inside an invisible box marked by painter's tape. They looked like they were about to be beamed to another dimension.

"Don't mind us," they laughed. "Just running tests for tomorrow's demo."

This group may have looked a bit crazy at that moment, but they were modeling the spirit of openness needed to develop disruptive ideas.

Ivani is using creativity to chart new paths in wireless with its Network Presence Sensing™ (NPS) technology. NPS can turn groups of wirelessly connected physical objects that were designed to sense people's presence into a network of state-of-the-art occupancy sensors. This has created innovative new possibilities and a very disruptive business model.

Matthew Wootton, Ivani's co-founder and chief technology officer, shared with me what he believes is the key to the company's rapid success.

"The whole problem definition process is just about everything when it comes to being innovative," he said. "You need to start here or you will not have the right focus for ideation."

Here's how to frame a problem with a compelling vision, clear parameters, and an open enough question.

 ## Creativity Starts with Clear Expectations

Even when thinking up new ideas to disrupt the way things are, we need constraints or we risk being irrelevant. When we look to tackle a problem with creative thinking, the challenge, vision, and expectations must be clear. If we don't have these, we risk wasting time creating the wrong product or writing the wrong book.

Imagine playing a sport where there is no out-of-bounds and there are no rules. That's why it is so difficult to watch an unfamiliar sport if you don't know the rules.

Without rules, fans wouldn't know what to expect and athletes wouldn't know how to train. One of the most common methods used to establish guidelines in business is a creative brief.

How to Write a Creativity Brief

Business consultant and author Todd Henry calls the balance between freedom and constraints *bounded autonomy*. In his book *Herding Tigers,* he writes: "Effective leaders establish clear principles for how they want the work accomplished, then allow their team members the space they need to work their magic."[2]

Designers and others in the advertising world are familiar with creative briefs, documents that guide the development of marketing and ad campaigns. Creativity briefs are similar, but they go beyond some creative briefs to specifically encourage new thinking.

When you are delving into a project that requires new solutions, take the time to fill out the details in the following brief. This will help you think through the project in detail and provide a clear framework.

If you're leading a team that you need to motivate, it can be helpful to complete this together.

Note that there are two parts to the brief. Provide plenty of opportunity for the team to ask questions and fill in missing details upfront. When they are still in the seeking possibilities stage, they should focus on the top of the brief. Don't shut down ideas based on the constraints. The bottom part of the brief should be used as an idea filter when finding solutions.

Tip **STAY ON TOP OF PROJECT CHANGES**

It's important to handle mid-project changes immediately and carefully. Once you set people working on a task that requires creative thinking, they tend to go deep.

CREATIVITY BRIEF

SEEKING POSSIBILITIES

Problem: State the problem here.

Vision: Turn the problem into a compelling vision statement, beginning with "It would be great if..."

Purpose: Why are we considering this right now? Why do we need it? What possibilities might result from us doing it?

Possibility Question: Turn the vision statement into a solvable possibility question, beginning with: "What might be all the ways...?" or "How might...?"

FINDING SOLUTIONS

Success: What does success look like? What outcomes do we want? What outcomes must we avoid?

Measurement: How will we measure success?

Resources: What resources (time, money, people) are we prepared to allocate? What's our budget?

Guidelines and Constraints: What must definitely be included in the solution? What must definitely *not* be included in the solution?

Stakeholders: Who do we need to get on board with our ultimate solution? In what ways can we start preparing the soil?

Timing: What is our timeline? Do we have a hard completion date? What's the pacing?[3]

DOWNLOAD TEMPLATE:

Creativity Brief

CHAPTER SUMMARY: THREE THINGS TO REMEMBER

→ It would be great if... these five little words are your ticket to crafting a compelling vision.

→ A solvable possibility question to invite new thinking + clear expectations is the secret to being more creative.

→ Constraints drive the need for creativity and freedom helps us get it done.

CHAPTER 8

How to Use Creativity to Make Meetings More Productive

"It is the supreme art of the teacher [manager!] to awaken joy in creative expression and knowledge."

—Albert Einstein

The best leaders are those who take responsibility for engaging the creative thinking of those with whom they work. This applies whether you are the official leader or just a person who wants to run better meetings or make your own work more impactful.

At a recent concert I attended at Caramoor Center for Music and the Arts, pianist Andrew Armstrong didn't assume that the audience was engaged simply because we were present and sitting in our seats.

Instead, he told a story using imagery and emotion to spark our interest. He went a step further, shared more history about the composer, and invited us to imagine our own stories as he performed the piece.

This pianist first activated the audience members' creative thinking to drive deeper engagement as he performed the piece.

Armstrong took a slightly different engagement approach for each piece he played that day, giving us opportunities to use humor, emotion, and visualization. It didn't matter that these three weren't every audience member's top strengths; as humans, we all have these skills to some degree and can connect with them.

How to Run a Meeting That Doesn't Suck

Picture your team members walking away from status updates with inspiration that lives with them for days afterward. Sound impossible?

The world of work desperately needs people like you who are open enough to consider this question and to take responsibility for designing meetings that engage.

Seventy-three percent of workers say they do unrelated work during meetings.[1]

Here is a simple structure for meetings that is designed to catalyze participants' interest from the get-go and keep them thinking about the topic after they walk out the door:

→ Motivate People to Engage

→ Open Opportunities to Dive Deeper

→ Spark Continued Thinking[2]

Example **STRUCTURING AN ENGAGING MEETING**

Your challenge: In an attempt to keep up with technology, your company has instituted several new Information Technology (IT) systems. Now employees are confused about how to use the different systems and they are wasting time duplicating efforts. You and other senior managers are tasked to develop a simple communique that helps people navigate the changes.

Creativity focus: For each meeting, you're going to choose one "aid" that will help you open up people's creativity. Options include:

- → visual elements,
- → humor,
- → the five senses,
- → empathy,
- → imagination, and
- → thinking from a new perspective.

For this meeting, you choose visual elements.

Step 1 **MOTIVATE PEOPLE TO ENGAGE**

Before the meeting or at the very start, pique people's interest with a funny video, cartoon, quote, interesting visual, unanswered question, or unique challenge.

Because you are focusing on using visual elements, you do a quick internet search for "confusing maps" and grab an image. Drag it into your email call to meeting and type:

"Our IT systems are starting to look like this [insert image] to employees. To Friday's meeting at 10 a.m., please bring a photo of something that seems visually confusing."

Do you think your colleagues will take note of this email? It's a bit different from what they're used to and you have already invited them to engage their original thinking.

Step 2 **OPEN OPPORTUNITIES TO DIVE DEEPER**

Use possibility questions to spark new thinking about a challenge.

Start the meeting by having people share the visually confusing pictures they brought. Lead a discussion. Why are they visually confusing? What would be better?

Now, it's time to go deeper and relate these images to the team's real challenge:

In what ways are these images like our IT systems?

By asking the above possibility question you open up space for new ideas. Remind yourself and others about the seeking possibilities guidelines, and have fun coming up with lots of responses.

Use this exercise to catalyze a discussion around the primary functions of each IT system. Clearly identify them and try to solve for the reasons people are confused about the uses for each system.

Step 3 **SPARK CONTINUED THINKING**

At the end of the meeting, your goal is to get your team to keep thinking about the challenge in new ways. This is called creative "incubation" and can lead to original ideas.

End the meeting with a question that people can take back to their desks to ponder further:

How might we depict our systems visually to make it easier for our users to understand the primary functions of each?

Ask each team member to further consider the problem and make concept sketches for possible solutions to the question. Keep it under the seeking possibility guidelines. They don't have to be designers, just thinkers, and there will be no judgment about their art. In the next meeting you'll share sketches and refine the ideas, then pass a final solution along to the design department to perfect.

How to Add a Visual Dimension to Your Meeting

You have probably heard about so-called visual learners, but do you realize that this skill is a native and important part of everyone's thinking?

There's a new genre that has encouraged individual visual note-taking, captured well in *The Doodle Revolution* by Sunni Brown and *The Sketchnote Handbook* by Mike Rohde. Taking notes with graphics and color helps us process and connect ideas.

You do not have to be an artist to embrace the idea of adding a visual element to meetings.

Stick figures and block letters count! Another option is to bring in a graphic recorder to scribe the meeting or workshop notes in live action. As ideas and questions unfold, they are captured visually so that all may see. Participants gain a big-picture perspective and see new connections with an added level of engagement.

I often bring graphic recorder Jane Harvey to participate in my talks. If she can't be there in person, I deliver my speech to her over Skype or Zoom and she creates a graphic recording that I can give to attendees as a handout, like the two panels below for a parent session on supporting creativity.

How to Inspire Creativity Even If Your Group Is Highly Technical

Mathematician-types are often discounted in a discussion about creativity, most often by the math-types themselves. When I train teachers in creativity principles, it's usually math teachers who say it just doesn't apply to them.

Having taught math courses myself, I say that creativity is almost more important since so many kids come to the subject with a fear. Creativity provides strategies to connect on a different level.

Data analytics folks sometimes feel they are exempt from creativity, too. But, as marketing research consultant Nadine Peterson has found, you will become quickly irrelevant if you think that way.

Peterson is a self-proclaimed math nerd, an expert in quantitative research. In recent years, she's found that storytelling and data visualization are key to making data more accessible and compelling to clients.

Math people really light up when we frame creativity as "working within constraints to find new solutions to problems." This is something they can relate to because they actually do it every day.

CANADIAN SPACE AGENCY ENGINEERS EMBRACE CREATIVITY

Creativity in government sounds like an oxymoron, doesn't it? How about creativity for engineers working in government? (Is there such thing as a double oxymoron?)

It's not an impossibility to Janice Francisco, CEO of innovation strategy firm BridgePoint Effect. When I do innovation transformations in companies, I like to work with Francisco in large part because of her background dealing with the stickiest of cultures— those bureaucratic behemoths called government. As Francisco knows, problems in government can become opportunities if we apply creativity.

Imagine Francisco is in a room with 14 middle level managers, mostly engineers from the Canadian Space Agency.

Their division is facing some challenges that need new thinking. This management team is considering training to prepare them to lead employees to engage in some form of the elusive "creativity and innovation."

One manager addresses the elephant in the room and says it can't be done. "We are just too constrained," they tell Francisco.

She replies, "There is no need for creativity and innovation if you're *not* constrained."

As she tells it, a light bulb goes off and the managers are newly open to proceeding with the training.

CHAPTER SUMMARY:
THREE THINGS TO REMEMBER

→ Creatively engaging meetings aren't fluff; they are designed to be highly productive.

→ Visual elements, humor, the five senses, imagination, and thinking from a new perspective are several creativity sparks you can use to engage people in meetings.

→ It's on you to provide a "hook" to make meeting participation purposeful and meaningful.

CHAPTER 9

How to Give Feedback on Creativity

As we improve our creativity, we develop our sensitivities to the world around us: our ability to spot problems, to understand others' challenges, and an overall general awareness.

When we use our creative thinking to bring forth new ideas, we tap into our innermost personal strengths.

This is vulnerable, hard work, and it reminds us that the way we give feedback to ourselves and others can make or break a project.

Most of us have worked with people that draw out the best in us and with others who shut us down. Now that we are asking people working in any job to bring their creative thinking to the table, it's important to get feedback right.

Why It Helps to Treat All People Like Designers

Once again, people in the design field have a proven track record of best practices since they have always been required to produce original work on demand.

Karen Krieger is an award-winning designer and worked for top firms like Saatchi & Saatchi before she founded her own marketing communications agency, Studio 210. She knows that to stay relevant in the marketplace, she needs all of her employees to come to work with their creative A-games in place. Though she has writers, architects, designers, and administrators working for her, Krieger treats them all like designers.

"As a creative director, I learned to look for designers' strengths," she told me. "What are their natural tendencies toward color, perspective, and balance? I do the same for my other employees, identifying strengths and building on them to support their best work and also to push them beyond what they thought was possible."

POPIT: A Powerful Framework to Improve Creativity

Giving productive feedback also starts with strengths. "You have to inspire them," Krieger said. "They need feedback to improve, but the feedback has to be given in a certain way, starting with the positives."

> **Definition:** **POPIT**
>
> POPIT is an acronym that stands for Positives, Opportunities, Problems, Inquiries, and Thoughts.[1] It is one of my favorite tools to encourage solutions-based thinking.

I've taught POPIT to entrepreneurs, CEOs, managers, teachers, parents, and teens; used this structure to grade assignments in graduate courses; and helped organizations incorporate POPIT into performance reviews. I've counseled people who are frustrated by negativity and resistance to new ideas to model this good feedback behavior with their bosses and co-workers.

This simple tool, when applied consistently, is a powerful driver of engagement, motivation, and continuous problem-solving. Its very structure is designed to push past the typical inertia of criticism into finding new possibilities.

Using POPIT as a feedback tool for our own and others' ideas creates change that starts to shift the culture in the workplace.

POPIT	
Positives	What's good?
Opportunities	What opportunities might result?
Problems	What are your concerns?
Inquiries	Turn problems into possibility questions: What might be all the ways...? How might we...?
Thoughts	What are all the new ideas to overcome the issues?

Case Study: Improving Customer Service Calls

Let's imagine that you manage customer service for a large online retailer. You've noticed that more and more customers have given feedback that customer service phone calls have left them feeling frustrated. Talking with your reps, it becomes clear that the mandate to get off the phone in under five minutes is taking a toll. They are on edge about the time clock running down and, even as they consistently solve customer issues within the timeframe, are coming off as hurried and impatient.

The obvious fix would be to remove the five-minute goal, but that's controlled by corporate far up the chain of command. You wonder, "What might I change for my team so that they can feel comfortable and relaxed on calls?" Usually the company doesn't directly share call metrics with the reps themselves, but you realize that if they were able to view their track record of meeting customer needs well within the five minutes, they could relax their approach. You also want them focused on positive communication, so you wonder how they might add customer delight to each call.

You approach the VP of operations with your two solutions:

1. to provide metrics to reps and

2. to add a goal of customer delight to each call.

This is his response:

Positives

"Great job thinking this through. I like that you have considered your own constraints, knowing that corporate is set on keeping the five-minute goal in place. You've thought about several aspects of this issue and proposed a two-pronged solution that addresses it."

Opportunities

"Your initiative might help us reverse this trend of dissatisfied feedback. It might also help restore engagement and levity in the call center—the reps have been pretty down and stressed out lately."

Problems

"One issue that I see is that we don't typically share call data with reps because we don't want them to compare themselves against each other."

Inquiries

"But, I'm willing to consider, How might we share call data without making it personal and competitive?"

Thoughts

You could take the time to seek new possibilities together, or he could send you off with the challenge question to think up ideas on your own and report back. Either way, the structure of POPIT keeps the process moving towards progress.

Rather than immediately say, "Nope, can't do that. It's not our policy to share the data," you are acknowledged for your new thinking efforts and encouraged to keep it going until you have a workable solution. After this process, you'll have a better solution whether it is slightly tweaked or totally revamped with new thinking.

 ## 9.4 Avoid Compliment Sandwiches

Some people might mistake POPIT for a "compliment sandwich." "It's just hiding the criticism within a couple of positives to make it softer and coddle fragile egos," they might say. That's not the intent of POPIT, which is designed to drive toward new thinking.

The very structure of POPIT provides a pathway to solve for weaknesses rather than get stuck ruminating within them.

Think about the differences between POPIT and Pros and Cons, an all-too-common way to evaluate ideas in business. POPIT makes way for a continuous flow of problem-solving and drives toward solution-oriented possibilities. With Pros and Cons, once you have a list there's no natural next step. Teams tend to get mired in debate.

In the paradigm of creativity that I teach, starting with strengths is paramount in every phase. Except in very rare cases when someone is truly acting defiantly, there's always a strength to be found.

Putting strengths first helps anchor the work going forward, again preventing us from getting lost in the issues and becoming consumed by the inertia of no.

Remembering the five steps of POPIT can feel awkward at first, but with practice it evolves into a natural way of responding. Work through it with your team or use it to evaluate your own ideas. While you're at it, try the POPIT method at home to respond to your kids' requests and your spouse's ideas. You will be amazed at how it catches on.

TOP 10 WAYS TO USE POPIT

1. Evaluate your own new ideas
2. Respond to suggestions
3. Give performance reviews
4. Meeting and event feedback
5. Develop solutions with a team
6. Grade student papers
7. Culture shift tool
8. Practice separating thinking
9. Structure a complaint
10. "Pre-work" for people who pose half-baked ideas

9.5 Your Work Sucks: Why Blunt Feedback May Not Work

I had an interesting debate recently with a colleague who was trained as an industrial designer. He told me that he feels he did his best work when teachers at design school essentially told him, "Your work sucks." He'd take the criticism and go back to the drawing board. He admitted that because teachers were blunt with him, he takes that approach with the undergraduate students he teaches.

Perhaps it depends on personality or context, but I am not a person who could treat people like that. I can always see a strength upon which to build. If you are seeking to be more creative at work, you are working mostly with people who have never been through the critique gauntlet. Saying, "Your work sucks" won't fly. It will probably shut them down. Go with POPIT.

9.6 The Real Secret to Offering Criticism without Having People Hate You

If you are a person who is known for critique, it might take a little doing to re-establish people's trust that your really are open to their new ideas. One approach is to be completely transparent:

"I know I tend to knock ideas and immediately find the problems in them. I've been working on changing that because I see that it's limiting your desire to come to me with new ideas. So, this is what I'm doing and you can help me by helping turn criticisms into possibility questions for further thinking."

HOW TO BUILD AND BREAK TRUST	
3 Ways to Build Trust	**3 Ways to Break Trust**
1. Recognize. Acknowledge what people do well.	**1. Ego.** Ask for new ideas but shut them down with your "better" ideas.
2. Employ strengths. Give work assignments that utilize strengths.	**2. Let critics rule.** Ask people to think differently, but fail to defend their new ideas from critics and naysayers.
3. Be grateful. Thank people for what they do.	**3. Ego.** Take credit for your team's work.

Teach POPIT to your whole team and institute it as the way of doing business.

Now, say you are trying to do this and since you tend toward being critical, your questions still come across as veiled criticism. My advice?

Dig deep and train yourself to lead with curiosity.

When you ask a question, try to ask it from a place of curiosity rather than skepticism. This will go far in helping your tone be authentic and trustworthy, rather than challenging.

How to Use Your Curiosity

If someone comes to you with a strategy that is clearly over-budget, be curious. "I am curious as to all the ideas you might have to make this idea less expensive?" I mean, aren't you curious? Wouldn't it be great if you could implement an awesome solution at a fraction of the price? With creative thinking this could be possible.

Tip 1 **THINK LIKE A BEGINNER**

It is often true that the more expert we become in our field, the less creative we are. We become mired in theories and procedures and "what's always been done."

When we have achieved master status there is less incentive to challenge the status quo—except that if we don't, we're bound to get stuck or become irrelevant.

How might you adopt a "beginner's mindset?"

Tip 2 **TALK TO PEOPLE UNLIKE YOURSELF**

An interesting project, started in Denmark during a weekend festival in 2000, has turned into an organization called The Human Library.

The "books" are people, and you "check them out" by reserving time for a person-to-person chat. The idea is to get to know personally the people about whom you might have negative preconceived notions: the homeless, Midwesterners, soldiers with PTSD, teen moms, nudists, and more.

There are chapters of The Human Library around the world, but all you need is to step out into your community and have a conversation with someone whose choices or background you may not understand. This will give you an opportunity to hone your genuine curiosity and question-asking skills.

Tip 3 **CALL FORMER COLLEAGUES**

Imagine executives calling their old contacts—people with whom they haven't spoken in many years—to ask for business advice. Now you do it.

In one study shared by David Burkus in his book *Friend of a Friend,* business executives overcame their resistance to doing this seemingly uncomfortable exercise. They reported that the advice they received from "dormant, weak ties"—acquaintances rather than close friends—was most novel and useful, the two main criteria that characterize creative ideas.

In another study, entrepreneurs launching new businesses—those whose ideas came primarily from weak ties—were more innovative and sought more patents and trademarks than those whose business ideas came from strong ties like close friends or family.

One reason for this is that our strong ties tend to have access to the same streams of information that we do. When we reach out beyond our close circles, all of a sudden we have access to divergent points of view.

Another factor is that strong ties come with the pressure of social conformity. We may be less willing to take risks on new ideas that might jeopardize our feelings of belonging amongst our tight-knit groups.[2]

What to Do If People's Ideas Really Do Suck

If you and your team are consistently producing ideas that are ho-hum and simply not helpful, bring in an expert to help you. All people and teams are capable of generating awesome ideas, but it's usually the process that falls short.

Consider an elementary school leadership team that I worked with. The school, which was building a new innovation center, had neighbors who were annoyed about the constant stream of construction traffic. Administrators wanted to improve the situation, but they couldn't figure out what to do. The ideas they'd come up with were drab and the head of school knew they wouldn't work.

Our team led them through a creative problem solving session (See Part Three for more on this) with the following four segments:

1. **Understand the problem.** The problem that was on the table was more clearly understood after we led the group through a process to dig deeper and create the right possibility question for the situation.

2.   **Seek new possibilities.** Every aspect of this session was carefully designed to draw out the group's best ideational thinking. Over 100 ideas were generated.

3.   **Find valuable solutions.** We taught the group to sort, analyze, and choose the best ideas. They selected a few final contenders, talked through them, and ultimately settled on one.

4.   **Get buy-in and plan for action.** The final idea? The school was going to have the kindergarteners (the most adorable people ever) harvest a bounty from the garden and deliver fresh vegetables to all of the neighbors. This was a far cry from other options they'd considered. Good luck staying mad when a bunch of cute little kids knock at your door with an offering of fresh vegetables! In this case, the kindergarten teachers were nearby and the group was able to get immediate buy-in.

**CHAPTER SUMMARY:
THREE THINGS TO REMEMBER**

→ POPIT is a robust feedback and idea improvement tool that stands for Positives, Opportunities, Problems, Inquiries, Thoughts.

→ POPIT is not about softening criticism. It is designed to keep active thinking alive as ideas are vetted and improved.

→ The secret to establishing trust so people will share their ideas with you is to replace full-on criticism with curiosity.

CHAPTER 10

How to Lead Creativity

Through multiple international studies of organizational leaders across industries, Gaia Grant from the University of Sydney found that effective leaders of innovation balance two seemingly paradoxical mindsets: Exploration and Preservation.

Some people have a decidedly "Exploration" preference. They tend to think broadly and make diverse connections to seek possibilities. Others have a decidedly "Preservation" preference. They tend to employ solution-focused thinking to drive implementation of set plans.

To be an effective innovation leader, you have to be able to navigate between both. You have to be ambidextrous.

 ## How to Become an Effective Innovation Leader

The chart below lists the four components that make up each of the two mindsets in Grant's Innovative

Change Leader Profile.[1] Can you estimate your personal preferences?

EXPLORATION	PRESERVATION
1 Freedom: Not being constrained by typical ways of thinking and doing	**Control:** Having discipline, ability to set clear parameters
2 Openness: Willingness to seek diverse perspectives and make connections	**Focus:** Prioritizing, placing attention on solutions
3 Collaboration: Sharing ideas, working effectively with others	**Independence:** Individual drive and passion to push through to practical outcomes
4 Flexibility: Exploring different potential applications	**Stability:** Testing and prototyping to narrow down to the best solution

To advance your own innovation leadership capabilities, start by developing all four Exploration dimensions: Freedom, Openness, Collaboration, Flexibility. Also develop one Preservation dimension: Independence.

VISIT ONLINE RESOURCES FOR:

Take the iCLi Survey to learn your innovation profile.

These are the five key areas where innovation leaders are strongest.

Tip 1 **CULTIVATE FREEDOM**

Develop your freedom by doing things differently. What are three things that your organization does now because "we've always done it this way"? Choose one and think up and try an alternate approach.

Tip 2 **HAVE OPENNESS TO THE UNEXPECTED**

Improv Everywhere is a troupe of actors, founded by Charlie Todd, that descends upon various venues in New York City to stage fun and harmless pranks. One of the group's most famous feats is "Frozen Grand Central," staged in the winter months of 2008, in which more than 200 actors froze in place for five minutes during rush hour in the busiest hub of Grand Central Terminal.

Each prank is filmed and the true entertainment comes from the reactions of unknowing bystanders who find themselves in the middle of a charade that (usually) surprises and delights them as they realize what is unfolding. If you watch my Top 10 Favorite Improv Everywhere videos, don't say I didn't warn you: you probably won't return to reading for a really long time.

VISIT ONLINE RESOURCES FOR:

Links to my Top 10 Favorite Improv Everywhere pranks.

Tip 3 FLEXIBILITY: MINIMIZE YOUR TRASH

Lauren Singer has rethought her entire lifestyle so that her full year's worth of trash can be contained in one small mason jar. And yes, ladies, that means she's even found an alternative to those fun monthly feminine products.

Since I learned about her work, I have been impressed with Singer's almost impossibly flexible thinking to overcome the inertia of trash.

What are five non-obvious things you can do today to reduce your own trash? Check out Singer's Trash is For Tossers website or her Instagram feed of the same name for inspiration. Even if she comes up with the ideas, it still takes flexibility for you to use them.

Tip 4 **COLLABORATION EXPERIMENTATION**

Do you tend to avoid collaboration? Maybe you feel like you end up doing all the work anyway, so why bother. Or you thrive working in a pair but not in a larger group.

Conduct an inventory of past collaborations to pinpoint what worked and didn't work. Then, draw up a list of your collaboration preferences and set up a couple of collaboration experiments that take them into account.

Tip 5 **INDEPENDENCE: DO DEEP WORK**

In his book *Deep Work,* writer and professor Cal Newport shares The Deep Work Hypothesis:

"The ability to perform deep work is becoming increasingly rare at exactly the same time it is becoming increasingly valuable in our economy. As a consequence, the few who cultivate this skill, and then make it the core of their working life, will thrive."[2]

Creativity *is* deep work. By honing this valuable skill, you have the opportunity to differentiate yourself and grow your creativity.

Here's how to implement this tip:

→ **STEP 1 - Set aside time in your week to focus on your own work.** Block out meetings with yourself for at least one hour but preferably for two hours or more.

→ **STEP 2 - Decide ahead of time what you will work on.** Choose something that requires new thinking. It can be interest-related or work-related, but the key is to give yourself enough time free of distractions.

→ **STEP 3 - Minimize that nervous, caffeinated energy** that keeps you hopping from task to task and screen to screen. Turn off all alerts, phones, texts, social media, and other distractions.

→ **STEP 4 - Try analog.** My most insightful thoughts emerge when I'm writing a rough draft with a pencil in a paper notebook. What analog approaches might you try to do your deep work off-screen?

→ **STEP 5 - Create a deep work routine.** Experiment with different times of day, lengths of time, and settings. What conditions are optimal for you? Read one of my favorite books, *Daily Rituals: How*

Artists Work by Mason Currey, for inspiration.
(As of this writing, Currey's second book was just
released: *Daily Rituals: Women at Work*). You'll
learn about the deep work routines of prolific
creators in history and realize that while there
are some commonalities, each person must craft
an approach that works for him or her. It doesn't
matter how you do it, just that you do it.

 ## Assess Your Creative Climate

Göran Ekvall's curiosity was sparked by trash. As an
industrial psychologist for Volvo in the mid-1950s he
helped develop a system to get feedback and ideas
from employees at all levels, including factory workers.
Soon he noticed that in some plants factory workers
contributed many ideas for workplace improvement
while in other plants the boxes were filled with candy
wrappers and cigarette butts.

Ekvall wondered, Why were some suggestion boxes
filled with valuable ideas from assembly line workers
while others were deliberately filled with trash?

This question got him hooked on studying the
psychological climates of organizations. Ekvall
pinpointed ten key dimensions that support creativity.[3]

CREATIVE CLIMATE DIMENSIONS

→ **Challenge**: Does work stimulate people to think in new ways?

→ **Freedom**: How free are people to choose the work they do and how they do it? Are they allowed to explore and experiment?

→ **Idea Time**: Is there time to generate ideas and think things through before having to produce?

→ **Dynamism**: Is there opportunity for constant activity and movement throughout the day?

→ **Idea Support**: Are new ideas and suggestions considered positively?

→ **Trust and Openness**: Do people feel safe offering different points of view?

→ **Playfulness**: Is it okay to have fun and smile?

→ **Free from Conflict**: Do people feel supported by colleagues and leaders, without back-biting?

→ **Debate**: Do people feel free to engage in lively debates about issues?

→ **Risk-taking**: Is it okay to suggest and try unproven ideas?

→ **Meaning**:* Is work generally meaningful?

*Over time working with Ekvall's 10 dimensions, I have added meaning to specifically call out this important aspect of work.

As you continue developing a possibility ecosystem, you can do a back-of-the-napkin assessment (based on Ekvall's seven decades of research on creative environments) to see how your group, team, or organizational climate supports creativity.

DOWNLOAD:
TEMPLATE

Get the full Creative Climate Workbook.
www.sparkitivity.com/strengthsspotter

The Key to Selecting One Area for Improvement

What if you completed the spider chart in the downloadable Creative Climate workbook and found that your environment has room for improvement on many dimensions?

In their book *Organizational Creativity,* Puccio, Cabra, and Schwagler suggest focusing on the top five dimensions emphasized by corporate groups:

- Freedom

- Idea Support

- Risk-taking

- Idea Time

- Debate[4]

Choose one dimension at a time and work toward improvement. As always, you can change the problem into a possibility question for creative attack.

For example, if your employees are strongly discouraged from taking risks, ask, "What might be all the ways we can shift so that employees feel comfortable taking risks?"

CHAPTER SUMMARY:
THREE THINGS TO REMEMBER

→ Effective innovation leaders achieve a balance between an exploration mindset and a preservation mindset.

→ A psychological climate that supports creativity is key to making innovation sustainable.

→ Freedom, support for ideas, risk-taking, time for ideas, and healthy debate are the top five most important aspects of climate, according to business groups.

PART THREE

Techniques For Being More Creative

CHAPTER 11

Creativity Models and Frameworks to Consider

There is a universal process that humans use to solve problems creatively across all disciplines.

You've been introduced to elements of this process piece by piece throughout the book and there is an important reason for this: when you adopt *any* of the practices, mindsets, or tools shared, you will improve your creativity. Many books on creativity in business lead with process, but I think it's more important to start with quick, manageable bites that you can incorporate into your life.

Now we can put it all together. Detailing the process out in stages, we can better understand how we solve problems, work to deliberately improve our approach, and teach others how to do it.

The Universal Creative Process

In its simplest form, the creative process has four main stages. Each of these stages calls both for seeking new possibilities and for finding valuable solutions.

Stage 1 UNDERSTAND: OBSERVE AND DEFINE THE VISION AND PROBLEM

(observe an issue; research; ask questions; create a vision; formulate the challenge; set success criteria)

Stage 2 IDEATE: GENERATE AND CHOOSE IDEAS

(generate new possibilities; use criteria to choose ideas)

Stage 3 EXPERIMENT: IMPROVE AND TEST SOLUTIONS

(draft the idea into a workable solution; prototype; get feedback; make improvements)

Stage 4 **IMPLEMENT: PLAN FOR ACTION**

(get buy-in; set a plan to activate the solution; and get it done)[1]

11.2 A Very Brief History of Creative Process

Historically, there are two predominant creative process strands: applied creativity and design.

APPLIED CREATIVITY

Creative problem solving is an applied creativity model that has its roots in the 1926 Wallas creativity process, one of the first known creative process models. Alex Osborn, the "O" founder of BBDO advertising agency, followed up with creative problem solving in 1953. There have been tweaks since then, but its essence is the evergreen model I just shared in the previous section.[2]

Over the course of its history, the creative problem solving process has been applied successfully across all industries to complex, strategic problems as a meta, multi-disciplinary model.

HUMAN-CENTERED DESIGN

Another creative process model was recently popularized by global design firm IDEO and Stanford d.school. Now called *design thinking* or *human-centered design*,[3] this approach emerged from the field of industrial design and was initially limited to product development.

Only more recently has it been applied to broader business challenges.

One of the central principles of design is its consideration of the end user. Empathy, or deeply understanding the needs and wants of the end user, is emphasized.

Because design thinking emerged from product development, there is also a focus on prototyping physical objects or experiences, getting feedback, and making improvements. It is a maker's process.

Case Study: How to Use Creative Process to Make Tattoos

When he was in early elementary school, Chuck Read used to get in trouble for drawing on other kids' arms and hands. For a while, he was even banned from using markers. Now he owns and operates Never Say Die, his tattoo shop in Harrisburg, Pennsylvania that is known for creating original art.

Read got into the tattoo business before it was trendy and stands firmly behind his trademark to create original artwork for clients. This is how the shop differentiates itself and why it has a dedicated core of repeat clientele. If you want a tattoo from Read, you can't just bring him a picture from the internet to replicate. As such, Read is saying "no" to the tendency toward sameness. His shop doesn't do it the way many shops do. He insists on original art, and that's why he goes through the steps of the creative process with every customer that comes in.

Step 1 **UNDERSTAND:** Read asks lots of questions about the client's vision, what he wants in a tattoo, why he's getting a tattoo, and where he wants it.

Step 2 **IDEATE:** Based on the client's interests, they think up possibilities for the tattoo design, color, size, and placement. The client chooses his favorite idea.

Step 3 **EXPERIMENT:** Read takes the rough concept, works out a design, and improves upon it. He shows the design to the client, the client suggests tweaks that Read then makes, and he shows it to the client for final approval.

Step 4 **IMPLEMENT:** Read now memorializes the design onto the client's body in the form of a tattoo. It's likely the customer is happy because Never Say Die has a loyal following of customers.

When we are used to doing something intuitively as part of our daily life or job, we may not realize that it follows a distinct process since it's so ingrained.

Before we spoke, Read hadn't thought of his work this way. But now, if he's so inclined, he can use the creative process to his advantage to meet goals he has—like coming up with more original art; spending less time perfecting a design that a client might change; or finding new questions to ask to get to the core of a client's vision.

The Creative Process Isn't Linear

It's true that the creative process is not always this straightforward and sequential, especially if we do it naturally without realizing we are moving through a process. But the linear visual is a good assist to help us analyze our thinking and make our creative process more deliberate.

IBM has depicted creative process as an infinity loop, representing it as a continuous, iterative process. This is probably more accurate than a straight line.

Michael Ackerbauer, an innovation coach in IBM's leadership development organization, took it a step further and overlaid the four creative process stages onto IBM's graphic. I like the continuous flow of this looping, which seems close to the iterative nature of the creative process.[4]

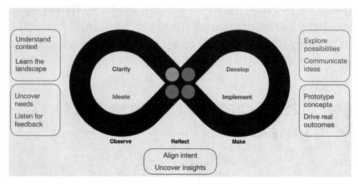

Image Copyright 2019 Michael Ackerbauer. Used with permission.

However it is depicted, we can use creative process to identify obstacles and use strategies to overcome them consistently.

Creative process is especially useful when working in groups; it provides scaffolding so we don't fall into the inertia of no such as indecisiveness, fear of judgment, or settling on an obvious idea.

11.5 Inside the Buzzwords: Agile & Lean Startup

The four creative process stages can be segmented into two separate categories, often called the front end and the back end of innovation.

Creative problem solving and design thinking help define or discover a problem and come up with killer ideas in the front end of innovation. Agile, Scrum, and Lean Startup streamline efficiency in refining solutions and getting them implemented quickly in the back end.

THE TWO SEGMENTS OF INNOVATION	
FRONT END (Understand & Ideate)	**BACK END** (Experiment & Implement)
Creative Problem Solving	Scrum
Human-Centered Design	Agile
	Lean Startup

Front-end and back-end innovation processes dovetail with each other. If you understand the tools and processes from each, you can mix and match for maximum benefit.

Our world tends to be hyper-focused on getting things done efficiently, and we tend to skip the robust front-end creative thinking. When we do so, we start out at a disadvantage.

This book is focused on powering up the underlying principles that can support fresh thinking in all stages of the process.

 # Case Study: Creative Problem Solving at Kimberly-Clark

Companies have customized innovation methods to their own business needs. Clayton Bunyard, research technical leader at Kimberly-Clark, has taught researchers how to incorporate creative problem solving principles and tools into the scientific and technical innovation frameworks commonly used in their R&D department, like Lean and the Scientific Method. He calls it "weaving a creative mindset into science."

"We have several innovation frameworks here and they vary by function," Bunyard told me. "Some R&D approaches tend to be analytical and aren't intentionally designed for divergent thinking. My goal is to help people see how they can deliberately weave creative problem solving tools into the frameworks they are already using. This helps build bigger, bolder ideas."

One senior leader told Bunyard that when continuous improvement programs were implemented in R&D, her people became so problem-oriented they had a hard time reframing their thinking into finding new opportunities. He knew how to fix it with creative process tools and techniques.

"Continuous improvement methods are great for what they are designed to do, but it's important not to over-extend them (or any other innovation method) beyond their purpose," Bunyard said.

As they continue to apply creativity tools at Kimberly-Clark, perhaps we can expect a future of self-cleaning diapers and invisible wipes![5]

How to Profile Your Preferences with FourSight

The most effective method I have found to help people learn how they navigate creative process and how to maximize innovation outcomes is the FourSight Thinking System.™ Fortune 500 corporations, non-profits, startups, universities, solopreneurs, teachers, and well-known organizations including Harvard, Nestlé, Starbucks, and the United Nations have had success with FourSight.

Dr. Gerard Puccio found two significant things in the foundational research from which FourSight was developed:

→ When faced with a challenge, humans engage in a universal creative process.

→ People have individual preferences across the four modes of creative thinking.[6]

The FourSight assessment helps you understand what kind of creative thinker you are and how you prefer to use your creativity to solve problems. The four basic preference profiles are clarifiers, ideators, developers, and implementers. Someone who likes them all is an integrator, and there are many additional preference combinations that help you pinpoint where your energy rises and falls while solving problems creatively.

Photo Credit: Doug Haight. Copyright FourSight, LLC. Used with permission.

My colleague Janice Francisco and I use FourSight as a practical strategy and first step to develop breakthrough thinking capacity on teams.

Unlike many assessments that give people insights about themselves, this one is about progress, growth, and forward change.

It reveals our cognitive preferences and gives us tools and strategies to be more comfortable working within all the stages of the universal creative process. We become more valuable thinkers individually and together.

FOURSIGHT IMPROVES PRODUCTIVITY AT IBM

In 2008, Michael Ackerbauer (the innovation coach in IBM's leadership development organization mentioned previously) spearheaded the use of FourSight across several teams. Later, the company conducted an internal study on growing and sustaining efficient innovation teams.

The study found that regardless of the innovation process being used (i.e., Agile, Lean Startup, Creative Problem Solving, Design Thinking, etc.), teams that had been trained in FourSight to know their creative process preferences and to use creative problem solving tools outperformed the teams that did not.

"When teams are aware of their preferences, conflict can be diffused or leveraged as creative tension, producing a potentially more synergistic result," wrote IBM research study lead and master inventor Casimer DeCusatis.[7]

One reason for improved relations like those the IBM teams experienced is the elimination of cognitive bias, our unconscious incompetence[8] that leads to team dysfunction. Statistics show we tend to reward people who have similar preferences to our own.

Let's say your team is full of people who love coming up with new ideas. Every meeting is like an ideation party. But there is one person on the team who wants to get things done. That buzzkill always breaks in and says, "Hey, guys, let's decide already and get this done." Can't you hear the groans?

But when the whole team is aware that everybody else prefers ideating and that guy prefers implementation, the situation becomes less personal. Instead, it can be viewed as a matter of preference and process.

The depersonalization helps to create a psychologically safe workplace for all and supports diversity in the workplace by putting everyone on the same playing field using the same language.

In this case, the group will now be aware that it needs to limit idea generation time and even leverage the teammate's zest for production in order to be more effective.

**CHAPTER SUMMARY:
THREE THINGS TO REMEMBER**

→ The universal creative process is a series of stages humans use to solve problems creatively.

→ Creative problem solving and human-centered design are two of the most-used creative process models.

→ We each have preferences about which stages of the process we like best: understand - ideate - experiment - implement.

CHAPTER 12

The Art and Science of Creative Problem Solving

Damien Newman, a former design strategist at IDEO, was working on a proposal for a client in the 1990s. He drew a quick squiggle to illustrate that they were about to jump into a process that might feel messy at first but would end up at a single point of clarity. This visual was so impactful it became known as The Design Squiggle,[1] a pretty accurate visual for the creative process in general.

Noise / Uncertainty / Patterns / Insights   Clarity / Focus

Research & Synthesis   Concept / Prototype   Design

The Process of Design Squiggle by Damien Newman, thedesignsquiggle.com.

Tools for Each Stage of the Process

When we begin with a problem, it often feels like a mess and may take a lot of work to even begin to unravel it. We may feel uncomfortable because we don't have all the answers or know exactly where we're going to end up.

This discomfort is a major reason some people avoid creativity, but the creative problem solving process makes it so much more palatable. We might find ourselves in the middle of a giant, confusing squiggle but we have steps to take and tools to use to get us out of it.

When you're planting a garden, building a set of shelves, or cooking a delicious meal, there is a certain order you follow and there are certain tools you need at certain times. In the following four sections, I'll make the process come alive with stories and give you a handful of the most impactful tools that you can use to get started in each stage of the creative process. You'll recognize several of them from earlier in this guide!

12.2 Understand the Problem

What's the most critical part of creative process?

Ideation is the obvious answer.

But to Einstein (or to the Yale engineering professor who probably said these words), it was understanding it—or figuring out the mess:

"If I had only one hour to solve a problem, I would spend up to two-thirds of that hour in attempting to define what the problem is."[2]

TOOLS TO UNDERSTAND BETTER

I was recently at a talk given by Andy Dunn, co-founder of the men's fashion brand Bonobos. He was asked how anyone could become an entrepreneur. His response? Notice something.

Dunn continued, saying that entrepreneurs observe and spend time thinking about problems they or other people have. Once you notice something, you're on the monkey bars and all you need to do is get to the next bar.

Tool 1 WHAT BOTHERS YOU?

First things first: you need a problem to solve. Start by writing down everything that bothers you, as you did in Chapter 1. These can be general life things, or irritants about a specific topic like your company's product.

Notice where people struggle or complain, whether they are co-workers, clients, or your kids. Write down all the problems.

Tool 2 UNDERSTAND THE PROBLEM WITH A QUESTION-STORM

Warren Berger is one of the world's present-day experts on asking questions. He is a proponent of "Question-Storming Sessions" to dig deep into a topic with a group. Berger's experience shows that when people are asked to brainstorm questions around a topic, rather than answers, profound insights emerge that clarify the right issue to be working on. He suggests an approach based on the work of the Right Question Institute:

1. **Set a focus.** Create a concise statement as a starting point, such as, "Our primary service is losing revenue year over year."

2. **Think up questions.** Use the seeking possibilities guidelines and generate ideas the way you would in

a traditional brainstorming session. In this case, he suggests ten minutes for starters. See Chapter 12.3.

3. **Make questions better.** Take a look at the list, combine duplicate ideas, and refine the questions. Turn them into possibility questions.

4. **Select favorites.** Each person or group marks one or two top questions. Questions that spark interest or discussion are contenders for the final selection.

Use this question as a basis for further ideation, visioning, and exploration.[3]

Tool 3 **DREAM A LITTLE DREAM**

The storyboard is a powerful visioning tool. All you do is take a piece of 8.5" x 11" paper. Fold it in half lengthwise and in thirds widthwise. You will end up with six sections.

Choose a problem that needs new thinking, and draw the current state of things in the first (top-left) section. Put in as much detail as you can, even if your drawing skills peaked in fifth grade like mine did.

Then, turn on your imagination and move to the last (bottom-right) section. If you could solve this problem, what would your future state look like? What would be happening? What would be possible? Imagine the future and draw it.

Finally, fill in the remaining four sections with a progression of scenes that represent what you must do to get from here to there.

As a last step, turn your problem into a vision statement. Capture the future state by beginning with: It would be great if...

DOWNLOAD TEMPLATE:

Full workbook of tools from this chapter.

Tool 4 **IDENTIFY PATHWAYS**[4]

Those four middle boxes of your storyboard probably have a bunch of roadblocks. Ask yourself: What might be all of the challenges that must be overcome to get from the current reality to my desired future state?

Write down all the roadblocks you can think of, stream-of-consciousness style. Then, use the question starters to turn them into possibility questions.

How might...? In what ways might...?

Roadblock	Challenge Question

Once you're done with that, take a look at all of the possibility questions and put a star by one or two that, if overcome, might yield the clearest path to progress.

 ## 12.3 Ideate Effectively

> *"Brainstorming, ironically, is a structured way of breaking out of structure."*
>
> —Tim Brown, *Change by Design*

My colleague David Eyman, a professor of creativity at Miami University in Ohio, recently received a call from city planners in a nearby town. One of its community buildings, used primarily as a senior center, was in disrepair. The town had money allocated to fix it but wanted to get input from the diverse perspectives of community members.

How might they improve the building so that it could continue to serve seniors but expand to be a more all-encompassing community center?

When Eyman and his university colleagues arrived for the seniors' ideation session, they met a packed room but the energy was low. The inertia of no wasn't budging and it was hard to encourage the group to seek possibilities. They mostly offered up complaints and stories.

Eyman knew he had to find a way to lighten the mood and shift the group out of the inertia of no. So he pulled out one of his favorite ideation tools: reverse brainstorming.

He tossed a new possibility question out to the group, following the contrarian questioning approach for this tool:

What might be all the ways to ensure that no seniors will ever again come to this building?

The room was ignited. Ideas started flying, beginning with:

Make us have to know how to use our smartphones to get in the door.

With that, everyone in the room laughed. The absurdity of the question eliminated the fear of putting out a "wrong" answer and there was freedom to think up possibilities. The seniors continued throwing out ideas, suddenly having fun:

- Take away our board games and replace them with video games.

- Require everyone who comes in the building to dress like a hipster.

Many of the ideas revealed that the seniors were not confident with technology. Valuable ideas began to emerge to address that fear.

As it turns out, Eyman himself has studied the "side effects" of brainstorming. He found that brainstorming provides benefits—such as group cohesion—that may even be more valuable than new ideas, as clearly illustrated by the seniors in suburban Ohio.[5]

Eyman used reverse brainstorming in this setting because he knew it would energize his group. There are many, many more divergent thinking techniques; each one works differently for different group dynamics and uses.

Technique 1 **REVERSE BRAINSTORMING**

The principle of reverse brainstorming is to play with the absurd. Instead of using a possibility question that includes the desired outcome (What might be all the ways to attract customers?), your question centers around the result that you don't want (What might be all the ways to make sure we never, ever get a new customer again?).

Technique 2 **BRAINWRITING**[6]

Some groups or individuals clam up when they have to say their ideas aloud. Brainwriting is an alternate tool, still collaborative but a quieter experience.

1. Set it up by writing the problem statement at the top of the page. Adhere nine square Post-it Notes onto each sheet of 8.5" x 11" paper, in a 3 x 3 grid. They do fit if you place them just right. Have enough sheets for each person in the brainstorming group, with a few extras.

2. Give each person a prepared sheet and have each person write one idea per Post-it Note across the top row.

3. When they are done with three ideas, they put the form back in the middle and take one that someone else has worked on (or the extra).

4. Add to that form by writing three more ideas, and return the form to the center.

This approach makes it easy to build on ideas other people have written.

DOWNLOAD TEMPLATE:

Full workbook of tools from this chapter.

**DOWNLOAD:
RESOURCE**

For a book chock-full of ideation and other tools, check out *Gamestorming* by Dave Gray, Sunni Brown, and James Macanufo

A NOTE ABOUT POST-ITS

Fun fact: Spencer Silver, inventor of the Post-it Note, and his wife, Linda, used to be my neighbors. It was before I was officially in the field of deliberate creativity so I didn't realize he was such a rockstar. I wish I had so I'd have more carefully guarded that giant pad of Post-its that he signed for me.

I get bored with the fact that I always use and recommend Post-it Notes. I do wish they didn't create extra waste. But they really are incredibly useful for group and individual ideation. I often sit at my desk with a stack of colored sticky notes to capture all of my ideas—for the concepts I wanted to include in this book; for my online publishing and Spark Report email newsletter topics; and for fun things to do with the family.

Not only are Post-its tactile, they can be easily moved around. That comes in handy for choosing ideas well.

Technique 3 **HOW TO CHOOSE IDEAS**

Let's assume that you finished your ideation session and have dozens of idea-filled Post-its on the walls. Now you shift into "finding solutions" mentality (using the guidelines) and try this simplified approach to choosing them.

→ **STEP 1 - Review the ideas and mark the ones that you think might be interesting, effective, and a bit surprising.** Be sure to filter the ideas through your objectives to ensure they solve the problem.

→ **STEP 2 - Move the ideas you chose into clusters to see how they connect with each other.** Categories will emerge as you move them. Once you see the categories, you will get an overhead view of your thinking.

→ **STEP 3 - Now it's time to find the essence of each cluster.** Restate the key ideas in each cluster, starting with this statement: What we see ourselves doing is.... Create a statement that is several sentences long to work out the general details of the idea. This will allow you to take promising but half-baked ideas and improve them.

→ **STEP 4 - POPIT (Yes, it's a powerful tool!)** When you really want to work through ideas, use POPIT to flesh them out in a robust and productive manner. See next section.

A Final Tip **HIRE A PRO OR GET TRAINED**

What if your brainstorming sessions are torture, always ending in team bickering and ideas that don't push the envelope?

A recent study showed that creative problem solving sessions with groups that had even a minimal amount of training in creativity tools and principles like those in this book generated three and a half times as many ideas as groups without training; these ideas were four times more original.[7]

Expert facilitators are artists. They can read a room and switch tools and techniques at just the right time to keep momentum going and make the most of the session.

If you have experienced even one expertly facilitated ideation session, you know what I'm talking about. It's like a nutritious meal for the mind.

There are several techniques that we professional facilitators use to ensure an ideation session goes well.

TOP 6 PRO FACILITATION TECHNIQUES

1. The facilitator does not generate ideas.

2. Create a possibility ecosystem in the room, including mindset, climate, approaches.

3. Insist on the seeking possibility guidelines during ideation, and the finding solutions guidelines when it's time to choose ideas.

4. Each person voices his or her idea aloud *after* it is written with black Sharpie on a Post-it Note.

5. Avoid praising specific ideas, but give the overall group continued encouragement.

6. Bring many different tools, catalysts, and strategies so you can pivot as necessary.

Experiment Continually

Robert Wang introduced Instant Pot 1.0 in 2010 after he was fired from the startup he founded. He sought to help people make healthy food fast, combining elements from slow cookers with elements from pressure cookers, which are quick but can be the most dangerous item in a kitchen. Since 2011, Instant Pot's sales have more than doubled every year and the company does no marketing.

What's the secret?

Instant Pot stays in perpetual prototype mode. As of this writing, eight years after the first one came out, there are nine models on the market. The company releases a new version every 12 to 18 months, based on customer feedback.[8]

PERPETUAL PROTOTYPE MODE

In a world of constant change, agility and flexibility are paramount. They begin with an experimentation mindset. When we view new business ideas as experiments to be tested and improved, the pressure to strive for one perfect end goal is released. We also get the opportunity to interact with end users to ensure we are creating something truly valuable. Prototype mode allows us to test the ever-changing marketplace in real time and pivot quickly if need be.

Tool 1 **3 QUESTIONS TO SHIFT INTO PROTOTYPE MODE:**

→ **Question 1.** How might I reduce the risk/exposure/ expense/time so that I'm comfortable viewing this effort as an experiment?

→ **Question 2.** How might I get early feedback so that I can make tweaks before finalizing the product?

→ **Question 3.** How might I shift the process into steps so I'm able to iterate the solution?

Tool 2 **IMPROVE YOUR IDEA WITH POPIT!**

One of the most powerful idea development tools is one you already know: POPIT. Once you are down to one or two solutions, write it at the top of the page in this format:

"What I see myself/us doing is..."

Complete the sentence with your solution. Then, work through the steps of POPIT to vet it.

Get Buy-In and Implement

Lisa Florczak invented the ice bike—and had it designed, manufactured, and ready for Buffalo, New Yorkers to rent and ride in fewer than eight months.

Lisa Florczak on her ice bike.

Intuitively, Florczak knew the importance of getting the buy-in that is critical to the implementation stage of the creative process. Which people will hop on board and who are potential blockers?

Before she dove too deep into pursuing her idea for a bicycle that skates, Florczak went directly to the Erie Canal Harbor Development Corporation. If she could create this thing called an ice bike, she asked, would they allow her to offer it for rent on the new Canalside ice rink they were building? The handshake approval she received gave her what she needed to proceed.

VISIT ONLINE RESOURCES:

Watch the ice bike in action.

But she didn't stop there. Throughout the design and development process, Florczak continued to get buy-in, from potential customers to indoor rink managers who were skeptical about allowing her to try her contraption on their ice.

PROTOTYPE MODE OVERCOMES THE INERTIA OF NO

Florczak maintained a mind frame of continuous learning and improvement: prototype mode! This mindset helped her get past the inertia of no. When doubt crept in, she reminded herself that she was simply working through an experiment.

Florczak is dedicated to keeping Ice Bikes of Buffalo manufacturing local so she can stop by and watch the process, make necessary changes, and guarantee quality. A continuous learning mindset like Florczak's minimizes the devastation of failure. If an experiment doesn't work, we can make changes and experiment again.

Tool 1 ASSISTERS AND RESISTERS[9]

Getting buy-in is one of the most critical parts of the creative process. You can have what you think is the most perfect solution in the world but if you can't get people on board, it won't work.

Here's an easy tool to help you figure out who will be

your best allies and to whom you might have to apply extra creative thinking to gain their buy-in.

1. Brainstorm a list of assisters and then a list of re-sisters. "What might be all of the people or circumstances that will assist or resist my project?"

2. Prioritize important assisters and figure out a plan to get them on board.

3. Prioritize important resisters. When you pinpoint a resister, turn the challenge they present into a possibility question so you can work on solving it.

Tool 2 IMPACT-COMFORT RADAR

How do you measure your new ideas against your own comfort level with them and the potential positive impact they may yield?

On the Impact-Comfort Radar, simply plot each viable idea in the quadrant according to where it rates in terms of both impact and comfort. Select the ideas that achieve a balance between both, or if the idea you think is best comes with a lot of discomfort, turn it into a possibility question and solve the challenge.

Tool 3 **TAKE ACTION!**[10]

There are many ways to create an action plan and you probably have your favorites. Perhaps you use spreadsheets or an online system to plan out your projects. I've included in the workbook download a simple planning chart so we don't lose sight of the fact that implementation is key to the creative process, but the best approach is to use your preferred way of planning for action.

CHAPTER SUMMARY:
THREE THINGS TO REMEMBER

→ Usually a problem to solve starts out looking like one giant messy squiggle.

→ We have tools at our fingertips that we can use in each stage of the creative process to help us move forward.

→ Prototype mode is a mindset that invites continuous learning and iteration.

CHAPTER 13

How to Measure the Impact of Creativity

"[Robots] will help us discover new jobs for ourselves, new tasks that expand who we are. They will let us focus on becoming more human than we were."

—Kevin Kelly, *The Inevitable*

Futurists agree that we're in for a greater tech takeover than most of us can fathom. They also say the tech explosion gives us an opportunity to get better at what we're designed to do: to be human.

What if growing our creativity is an exercise in growing our humanity?

It is. Creativity is one of our most distinctly human qualities. It relates to intelligence, spirituality, insight, intuition, courage, respect, humility, and yes, love.

Growing our creativity is growing a different type of intelligence than IQ—our creative intelligence. It is the awakening of multi-dimensional human capabilities.

When we grow our creativity, we increase our humanity and our impact.

Even the smallest effort at growing our creativity can send forth a ripple that moves a community closer toward being a possibility ecosystem. Though a ripple disrupts the surface of a calm, placid lake, it serves to regenerate the waters so they don't stagnate.

When we consistently apply any of the ideas in this book, we start regenerative ripple effects in our own ecosystems.

How can you possibly measure the ripple that begins when someone at work asks you a possibility question, which reminds you to ask your kid a possibility question, which solves a major challenge and averts a disaster at school?

Case Study: Aligning Your Team

Paul Golaszewski is the national sales director for Waterworks, a luxury home fixtures company. As the manager of over 150 salespeople in remote teams across the country, Golaszewski is constantly making sure that teams are aligned around the same goal.

"Do we agree on what success looks like?" is his key question.

This anchors the work and keeps people from getting off track. Success is carefully defined at the outset of each project.

Measure Creative Impact

When we are looking to measure the impact of creativity, we can take a similar approach. We can measure aspects of impact, but we can't measure all impacts of creativity at once.

FIVE CATEGORIES OF POTENTIAL MEASUREMENT[1]

1. Individual Metrics

2. Team Metrics

3. Project Metrics

4. Portfolio Metrics

5. Ecosystem Metrics

BEGIN WITH GOALS

In an era of big data, it's tempting to measure anything and everything. Instead, we can take a goals-focused approach to assessing creative impact. The main purpose is to ensure we're on the right track.

A mix of qualitative and quantitative data can be helpful. Qualitative data is observation-based and doesn't involve numbers.

To quantitatively evaluate progress, you can create what Tristan Kromer from Kromatic calls a metrics-driven experiment based on your specific goals. He suggests the following four steps.

Tool 1 **CREATE A METRICS-DRIVEN EXPERIMENT**

→ **STEP 1 - Learning Goal.** What are you trying to learn?

→ **STEP 2 - Measure.** What data might help you answer your learning goal?

→ **STEP 3 - Plan and Execute.** What will you do to gather the data? Make a plan and try it.

→ **STEP 4 - Evaluate.** Reflect on gathered data.

Below is an example of two measurement experiments based on the goals of this book.

Example A **MEASURE YOUR QUESTIONING SKILLS**

STEP 1 - LEARNING GOAL

One goal of this book is to help you grow creativity by asking possibility questions that enhance your ability to turn roadblocks into solvable problems. In this experiment, let's specifically measure if you are increasingly using this skill. Ask yourself:

Am I asking more possibility questions day-to-day?

STEP 2 - MEASURE

It would be useful to get a count of how many possibility questions you actually ask yourself and others over the course of a day and week. What might be all the times you use "what might be all the" or "how might" to begin your questions?

STEP 3 - PLAN AND EXECUTE
Keep a daily tally of the number of times you remember to ask a possibility question instead of getting stuck in a dead-end challenge or criticism.

STEP 4 - EVALUATE
Are your numbers increasing?
What are you doing well?
What can you do more of?

Example B MEASURE THE IMPACT OF YOUR QUESTIONING SKILLS

STEP 1 - LEARNING GOAL
Is asking possibility questions making a positive impact?

STEP 2 - MEASURE
It would be useful to understand what happens after you ask each possibility question.

STEP 3 - PLAN AND EXECUTE

As you keep track of the number of times you ask possibility questions, also write down the effect of those possibility questions.

What happened after you asked them?

Count the number of ideas generated, or the number of times you or another became unstuck.

STEP 4 - EVALUATE

Are you finding new ways forward?
Are those you interact with finding new ways forward?
Are you opening up thinking pathways for new ideas?

ARE IDEAS IMPROVING IN THEIR CREATIVE MERIT?

One result of using creative process consistently is generally an increase in original, useful ideas.

Originality is one of the easiest dimensions of creativity to measure. Something that is original is statistically rare. It may not be 100 percent original to everybody in the universe, but it is original in the context of known information.

Are your ideas same-old, same-old, or do you have a growing number of ideas that are fresh, different, and a little bit scary? Here's a way to evaluate them.

Tool 2 **CREATIVE PRODUCT ANALYSIS MODEL (CPAM)**[2]

The CPAM is an empirically tested model designed by Susan Besemer to set a universal standard in the evaluation of creative products, which can include ideas, physical objects, theories, etc. While subjective, the measure has proven to be reliable and valid when used by multiple experts in a field to evaluate products.

You don't have to set up an official scientific study to use this tool, but you can ask the following questions as a guide to consider the creative elements of a product or solution. To set up an evaluation (roughly) according to CPAM standards, get a group of people with similar industry expertise to separately evaluate your product using these questions.

1. Novelty

- → Is it unusual, or infrequently seen among people with similar backgrounds and training?
- → Does it include new materials, concepts, or processes?

2. Resolution

→ Does it meet the needs of the situation?
→ Does it have clear, practical applications?
→ Is it user-friendly?

3. Style

→ Is it well-crafted?
→ Do all parts work well together?

13.3 The Ripple Effect of Being More Creative

Starting a ripple effect of creativity is the same as starting a ripple in a pond—we have to be aware that we can toss a stone in the water in the first place. We also need access to the stones. The strengths, language, tools, and processes in this book are your stones. Begin with any of them. In fact, you already started when you picked up this book.

This work will impact your own life first. No one else may even notice as your thinking shifts into a mindset of possibility. Maybe you already have this mindset, and if so, it will be strengthened. You will have the language and strategies to model your approach as you work with others. With this applied practice, your ripple effect will grow. You will be able to toss multiple stones simultaneously and achieve more impact.

As my friend André-Paul in the shoe department demonstrated, life can get better for everyone when people seek to improve their own creativity first. André-Paul's ripple effect didn't stop with me; the women at my keynote got a glimpse of the possibility that they can wear comfortable shoes, too.

The great thing is that you don't have go to extremes to be more creative. So much of growing our creativity is understanding what it is, how it works, and how we approach it individually.

Simply becoming more aware of the two dimensions of creative thinking (seeking new possibilities and finding valuable solutions) and how to more robustly exercise them, you will experience creative growth. This will then gently ripple out into your ecosystem through your relationships.

**CHAPTER SUMMARY:
THREE THINGS TO REMEMBER**

→ Being more creative helps us be more human.

→ It's probably impossible to measure all of creativity, but we can measure aspects of it.

→ Focus on impact when you create your own measurement experiment to help check creative progress.

CHAPTER 14

How to Get Started

Years ago, when I was leading a client through a creative process facilitation, the light bulb suddenly went off for me. I understood why using deliberate principles and process is the secret formula to sustainable creativity:

Process gives us a way to start, a road that leads us forward even when our thoughts feel stuck.

This client, a serial entrepreneur, was at a career crossroads. He'd founded and sold several successful companies and had to decide what to do next. His most recent 23-year gig had been successful, but he wanted a new start that was more deeply satisfying. The client was so open to a flood of potential possibilities that his thoughts were in a tangled mess, like The Design

Squiggle. He didn't know how to even begin. Applying creative problem solving helped him dream, think, focus, and move forward.

We gathered a team of confidants together to help him clarify his vision. Ultimately, he settled on this focus: It would be great if . . . I could have a career that makes me excited to get up in the morning because I am doing good for the world.

From there, the group members helped him come up with all of the potential possibilities in a number of interest categories. They also helped vet and choose the ideas using criteria he had laid out. Very soon after our session, the client was ready to roll, moving forward to establish several new ventures that fit within his vision.

That's when I saw the power of process to free people to move forward with possibilities.

Most challenges start off as a tangle of thoughts, facts, and limitations. Simple principles like separating the act of imagining and seeking possibilities from the act of choosing and analyzing solutions; creating vision statements; stating challenges as possibility questions; and using tools within the stages of the universal creative process give us a pragmatic way to jump in and start unraveling the threads.

When we start to do this habitually, it feels less like process and more just "what we do."

 ## 14.1 What Not to Do

So how can you get started using the ideas in this book without feeling like an imposter?

Here's what not to do.

Don't start spewing buzzwords without doing the work. Real creativity gets a bad rap when fakers say things like, "OK, let's be creative now!" in one breath and shut down every new idea in the next.

To be effective at creating possibility ecosystems, you must do the work yourself. You must model what you know of best practices.

DEVELOP A POSSIBILITY ECOSYSTEM LIKE A GOOD PARENT OR TEACHER

1. Model best practices.

2. Draw out strengths.

3. Thank people for what they are doing well to encourage more of it.

4. Provide opportunities for practice.

Two Approaches to Begin

As you begin doing this work, you can choose to do it out in the open, or you can be a stealthy creative ninja. It all depends on your personality and circumstances.

TWO ROUTES TO APPLYING CREATIVITY PRINCIPLES AT WORK

1. **Overt**. Integrate these ideas into the work you are doing. Come right out and tell people you've learned some methods that you'd like to try to in order to facilitate growth and innovation.

   Use this method if:

   → You work for yourself (duh). Simply start applying the techniques and tools to your work.

   → You are tasked with seeking methods to help your team solve problems better or collaborate more effectively.

→ You are the team lead or the boss and you know it's important to create a possibility ecosystem to keep your team working at its best.

→ You work in an environment where people are naturally open to new ideas that help them grow.

2. **Covert**. Start integrating some of the tools and language into your individual work, without referencing what you're doing.

Use this method if:

→ Your team or organization is set in its ways and resistant to change.

→ You're unsure about how people will react if you go overt. Test it out quietly first.

→ Your organization talks "creativity and innovation" but avoids commitment to making it real.

→ You don't feel an overt approach would go over at this moment.

STEALTH CREATIVE PROCESS AT WORK

One of my clients is the CEO of a small, but successful tech firm. He is a longtime entrepreneur and intuitively uses creativity principles. He's what I call a natural creative thinker. However, at times, his approach seems diametrically opposed to those of the newly minted MBAs in his company.

When I first gave him a crash course in creative leadership, I listened carefully to his present practices. Then I connected what he already does very well to the language of creative process, a language that even resonates with the most analytically trained MBA.

He decided to use the covert approach to drive much-needed innovation. We designed some possibility questions to integrate into the customer support call center, he started using POPIT in his interactions, and he learned several additional tools to help connect his natural creative process with that of his employees.

Soon after this, the company came out with a much-needed innovation to set it up for this next iteration of the future.

On Being Humble

As Kevin Kelly writes in *The Inevitable,* we are living in a world in which everything is in a flowing, changing state. This flux turns us into continuous learners.

Kelly points out that we are all "newbies" all the time. Yet, after we learn something we tend to believe we're expert and subconsciously block further learning.

For example, I am still learning about creativity. As I was writing this book today, I came across an intriguing new definition of creativity that I didn't know yesterday. I'd love to hear from you, too. How do you define creativity? How do you apply it? What practices can you share that would help me improve?

Being a continuous learner takes a great deal of humility. So does creativity. There's always missing information and the answer is not pre-defined and obvious.

To get more comfortable always being a newbie, ask more questions. Think of yourself as a learner, not an expert. Check your ego at the door. Think you're the most creative person ever? Realize the benefits of working with others, building on ideas, and listening for how to improve and for what to solve.

Without humility, creativity doesn't work. If you think you're better than your team, you will never create a possibility ecosystem. They will not trust you. You will get stuck.

 ## What If You Get Stuck?

Too many ideas.

Not enough ideas.

Your idea didn't work.

Not sure where to begin.

Sometimes when I simply don't know what to write, I take out a stack of Post-its, remind myself to get into a fun mindset where all ideas count, and start writing ideas on the notes. This is an example of leaning on process to get unstuck.

Turn to the pages of tools that align with the stages of the creative process; pick one that seems to fit where you are in your challenge; and work it through using that tool.

You can also lean on creativity principles, like turning challenges into possibility questions, or *It would be great if...* statements, or replacing *no* with *why*.

If you've been working long hours and feel discouraged about moving forward, take a break. Getting outside in nature is especially helpful to shift thought. So is taking a shower. You can even get waterproof paper and pencils to write down the thoughts that pop into your head while you bathe.

This book is designed to support you as you go about your creative journey. Go online and get the resources designed to help you out; use this guide as a reference; or reach out to me directly at inspired@sparkitivity.com and I'll help you, or connect you to just the right person in my own ecosystem of possibility: a world-wide network of the top professionals in the fields of creativity and innovation.

14.5 Ready, Go!

As you set out on this journey, remember that being creative is not about arts and crafts, but it's about robust thinking. It's an action of mind that is characterized by movement, shifting, connecting, and breaking past mental barriers. Just as you can choose to get off the couch and exercise, you can choose to operate in this possibility-seeking mindset.

> *"If you become someone who is uncomfortable unless she is creating change, restless if things are standing still, and disappointed if you haven't failed recently, you've figured out how to become comfortable with the behaviors most likely to make you safe going forward."*
>
> —Seth Godin, *The Icarus Deception*

But when you choose to go forward with creative thinking, remember that the inertia of no will do everything to get you to stay seated. It will jump up and down in your brain and say you don't have time, you're a fake, you don't have what it takes.

Just ignore it. Prove it wrong. You've decided to take the creativity leap and you can work diligently through the challenges.

We need you to use your creativity, to lead creativity, to make possibility ecosystems wherever you go.

History is riddled with situations that resulted from a lack of imagination. In the present, we are constrained by myths and limitations that creative thinking can help us break down so we can get unstuck in our personal lives and as an interconnected world. You never know how far your ripple will go.

CHAPTER SUMMARY:
THREE THINGS TO REMEMBER

→ Don't be a faker. Do the work it takes to think creatively.

→ Lean on process when you feel stuck.

→ Humility helps creativity flow.

Gratitude

Gratitude, like curiosity, opens the door to possibility. I am grateful to so many who helped deepen and expand the insights in this book.

BEGINNING

Thank you to:

Jenny Blake, for introducing me to Rohit and his fascinating work on your Pivot Podcast.

Rohit Bhargava, for asking that this book be written.

Joan Smutny, for believing in my writing years ago before I knew I had it in me.

Jeff and CJ, for supporting me every step of the way, for taking Saturday adventures so I could work for crazy 13-hour stretches, and for always being ready to celebrate!

Pam Slim, for supporting the shift.

Justin McKinney, Amy Zipper, Kristen Bennie, Pam Simmeth, Charlie Youngblood, Troy Schubert, Nacho Arrizabalaga, Karen Krieger, Matt Hall, Rick Pollak, Elizabeth Hayduk, Matthew Wootton, Andrew

Armstrong, Nadine Peterson, Chuck Read, Lisa Florczak, Paul Golaszewski, and (the late) Dixie Hudson for interviews that helped determine the book's content.

GROWING

Thank you to:

Dad, for the inertia of no.

Nicole Crane, for being my deep-soul sounding board and for thinking of wolves—the idea that broke through the inertia of no.

Dad, Mom, and Jeff, for word-smithing with me until late into the night.

Jeff, for reading the first (and horrible) draft.

David Eyman, for vetting my ideas through your vast reservoir of knowing one thing about everything.

Jane Harvey, for giving me a collaborative boost throughout the development phase.

Janice Francisco, for demonstrating the power of generosity and partnership.

Gaia Grant, for sharing your cutting-edge research and answering my perpetual questions.

Clay Bunyard, for expert insights and taking the time to check my facts.

Jennifer Quarrie, for reading a bad first draft under pressure.

Roger Firestien, for being an incredible historian to help properly source the ideas in this book.

Gerard Puccio, for clarifying research and support.

Macker, for explaining the loop over breakfast at (the late) KR Cafe and for training collaborations.

Charlie Garland, for your solid research, insights, and collaborative spirit.

Carrie Smith, for your enthusiasm to apply the ideas in this book immediately after you read a draft.

Gretchen Gardner, for thoughtful questions and editing feedback that pushed me into truly non-obvious territory.

SHARING

Thank you to:

Allison Lancaster, for being the perfect teammate at the perfect time.

Marnie McMahon, Jessica Angerstein, and the team at Ideapress for your production and design expertise that is shepherding this book into the world.

Every reader and supporter who has read and shared this guide!

REFERENCES

Endnotes

Chapter 1

1   Answer to The Masked Man - The man with the mask
    was the catcher in a baseball game; the other man was
    a base runner. Nathan Levy, Stories with Holes Volume
    1 (Hightstown, NJ: N.L. Associates, 2005) 2. Explore
    additional titles here: http://www.storieswithholes.com.

2   Creativity Includes Two Types of Thinking - Seeking
    new possibilities refers to divergent thinking and
    finding valuable solutions refers to convergent
    thinking.

3   Spark Possibilities Guidelines - One of the classic
    books in the field of creativity, by the inventor of
    brainstorming: Alex Osborn, Applied Imagination,
    (New York: Charles Scribner's Sons, 1953). Props to
    David Eyman for inspiration on "Hone Your Ideas"
    guideline #3: "Does it scare you just a little?"

4   Proof That You Were Born Creative Study - The most
    readable write-up of the Land study can be found in
    George Land and Beth Jarman, Breakpoint and Beyond
    (New York: HarperBusiness, 1992) 153. This book gives a
    fascinating look at creativity, change, and possibility.

Chapter 2

1   Nuclear Shock Wave Information Growth - Kevin
     Kelly details the patterns of change in his book,
     demonstrating that we live in a continuously flowing
     state. His view of the future is less dystopian than
     others, and he emphasizes that technology will help
     us all learn how to "become more human." I highly
     recommend: Kevin Kelly, The Inevitable (New York:
     Penguin, 2016) 258.

2   US Patents - You can find every possible stat about
     patents on the United States Patent and Trademark
     Office website, https://www.uspto.gov.

3   Wolves in Yellowstone - Scientists have studied
     the Yellowstone ecosystem and have determined
     that wolves were a catalyst to the changes. If you
     want to get into the science, check out this paper:
     Peterson, Vucetich, Bump, and Smith, "Trophic
     Cascades in a Multi-causal World: Isle Royale and
     Yellowstone," Annual Review of Ecology, Evolution,
     and Systematics 2014, 45: 325–345. If you want to
     watch the much simplified video, search "How Wolves
     Change Rivers" or go to https://www.youtube.com/
     watch?v=NGhOzGbpEmI.

4   Shinola Creates Artisanal Watches - Shinola's story can
     be found in David Sax, The Revenge of Analog (New
     York: PublicAffairs, 2016) 158. View the Shinola watch
     factory tour video here: http://www.businessinsider.
     com/shinola-watch-factory-tour-2014-3.

Chapter 3

1   Creativity for Everybody - Kathryn P. Haydon and
       Jane Harvey, Creativity for Everybody (New York:
       Sparkitivity, 2015).

2   Where Did These Thinking Strengths Come From?
       - This survey is based directly on the work of E. Paul
       Torrance. While his research on these divergent
       thinking strengths dates back to the 1960s, the best
       book to learn more is: E. Paul Torrance and Tammy
       Safter, Making the Creative Leap Beyond (Amherst, MA:
       Creative Education Foundation Press, 1999).

3   Metacognition Quote - Puccio, Mance, and Murdock,
       Creative Leadership: Skills That Drive Change
       (Thousand Oaks, CA: Sage, 2011) 72.

Chapter 4

1   Imposter Syndrome Study - Belgian researchers
       surveyed over 200 professionals and published
       this study: Jasmine Vergauwe, et al., "Fear of Being
       Exposed: The Trait-Relatedness of the Impostor
       Phenomenon and its Relevance in the Work Context,"
       Journal of Business and Psychology 2015, 30: 565–581.
       https://link.springer.com/article/10.1007/s10869-014-
       9382-5.

2   Gallery of Quotes -

       Maya Angelou: https://bookriot.com/2017/11/22/
       quotes-about-impostor-syndrome/

       Tom Hanks: https://www.npr.
       org/2016/04/26/475573489/tom-hanks-says-self-
       doubt-is-a-high-wire-act-that-we-all-walk

Lady Gaga: Gaga: Five Foot Two documentary https://www.netflix.com/title/80196586

John Steinbeck: https://www.entrepreneur.com/article/303423

Penélope Cruz: https://www.cbsnews.com/news/a-visit-with-penelope-cruz/

Tina Fey: https://www.independent.co.uk/arts-entertainment/films/features/tina-fey-from-spoofer-to-movie-stardom-1923552.html

Chapter 5

1   Jia Jiang's Rejection Therapy - "What I Learned from 100 Days of Rejection" - https://www.ted.com/talks/jia_jiang_what_i_learned_from_100_days_of_rejection; DareMe app based on Rejection Therapy: https://www.rejectiontherapy.com/100-days-of-rejection-therapy.

2   Possibility Questions - I termed these types of questions "possibility questions" after Anna Craft's "possibility thinking": Anna Craft, Creativity Across the Primary Curriculum: Framing and Developing Practice (London: RoutledgeFalmer, 2000). Sidney Parnes was the first to suggest using specific phrases that invite idea generation instead of idea blocking: Sidney Parnes, Creative Behavior Guidebook, (New York: Scribner, 1967). This is a technique that was also adopted and has been shared widely by IDEO through its application of design thinking. Roger Firestein (the man who should be in the Guinness Book of World Records for having taught more people the creative problem solving process than anyone else in the world) and his colleagues coined "What might be all the . . . ?" in: Blair Miller, Jonathan Vehar, Roger Firestien, Sarah Thurber,

and Dorte Nielsen, Creativity Unbound: An Introduction to Creative Problem Solving (Buffalo, NY: Innovation Systems Group, 1999) 51. I highly recommend this book if you want a practical guide to creative problem solving process.

Chapter 6

1   Possibility Ecosystems - The 4 Ps Model of Creativity is one of the most time-tested and simple ways to understand how creativity works from a systems standpoint. People, Process, and Press (environment/culture/climate) play upon the others to influence the Product, or outcome. Mel Rhodes, "An Analysis of Creativity," The Phi Delta Kappan 1961, 42: 305–310.

The 4Ps model has evolved into the Creative Change Model, put forth in: Puccio, Mance, Switalski, and Reali, Creativity Rising: Creative Thinking and Creative Problem Solving in the 21st Century (Buffalo, NY: International Center for Studies in Creativity Press, 2012).

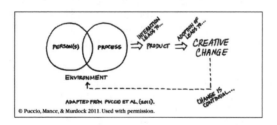

Image Credit: Jane Harvey, *Creativity for Everybody*

2   K.H. Kim Quote - Kyung Hee Kim, "Measurements, Causes, and Effects of Creativity," Psychology of Aesthetics 2010, 4: 131–135.

3   Engagement -

Gallup Report: https://www.gallup.com/workplace/238079/state-global-workplace-2017.aspx?g_source=link_newsv9&g_campaign=item_225752&g_medium=copy.

McKinsey Survey: https://www.mckinsey.com/business-functions/organization/our-insights/attracting-and-retaining-the-right-talent.

Chapter 7

1   It Would Be Great If... Miller, Vehar, Firestien, Thurber, and Nielsen, Creativity Unbound: An Introduction to Creative Process (5th Ed.), (Evanston, IL: FourSight, LLC, 2011) 63.

2   Bounded Autonomy - This book is targeted to anyone who leads teams of "creatives," but is especially helpful to creatives who have been promoted to leadership roles: Todd Henry, Herding Tigers: Be the Leader that Creative People Need (New York: Penguin, 2018).

3   Creativity Brief - The Success, Measurement, and Resources categories on this brief were influenced by Tim Hurson's DRIVE tool. This tool and other rigorous creativity-in-business tools can be found in: Tim Hurson, Think Better (New York: McGraw Hill, 2018).

Chapter 8

1   Bad Meetings Stats - You don't need these stats to know
    how unproductive most meetings are, but they can
    help you make your case for creativity! https://www.
    inc.com/chris-matyszczyk/here-s-proof-that-most-
    of-your-meetings-are-a-waste-of-time.html.

2   Structuring an Engaging Meeting - This structure is
    based on the Torrance Incubation Model for Teaching
    and Learning. This model has gained traction in
    education recently, as the need for creative thinking
    is more broadly acknowledged. Its principles apply
    equally well in business, since business requires
    continuous learning and creativity. This model
    was originally proposed in: E. Paul Torrance, "An
    Instructional Model for Enhancing Incubation," The
    Journal of Creative Behavior 1979, 13: 23–35.

Chapter 9

1   POPIT - This tool was developed in the early 1980s by
    Diane Foucar-Szocki, Bill Shepard, and Roger Firestien.
    The original tool was called PPC—Pluses, Potentials,
    and Concerns, and has since expanded to PPCO (to
    include Opportunities). I have changed the acronym to
    POPIT to make it fun.

2   Calling Former Colleagues - David Burkus used the
    latest research on networking to pinpoint eleven
    universal principles that, if followed, can help us grow
    our productivity and creative thinking potential as we
    work better with our network: David Burkus, Friend
    of a Friend: Understanding the Hidden Networks that
    Can Transform Your Life and Your Career (New York:
    Houghton Mifflin Harcourt, 2018).

Chapter 10

1   Innovation Change Leader Profile - Gaia Grant and Martin Dowson, "Leading Innovation in Ambiguous Contexts: Paradoxical Innovation Leadership Orientations for Future Sustainability," 35th European Group for Organizational Studies (EGOS) Colloquium, Edinburgh, Scotland, 5 July 2019.

Gaia Grant, "From Detecting Dichotomies to Navigating Dipoles: A Theoretical and Practical Model for Identifying Paradoxical Innovation Leadership Orientations," 34th European Group for Organizational Studies (EGOS) Colloquium, Tallinn, Estonia, 7 July 2018.

2   Deep Work - Cal Newport, Deep Work (New York: Grand Central Publishing, 2016) 14.

3   Creative Climate Dimensions - Göran Ekvall,"Creative Climate," Encyclopedia of Creativity Volume I, A-H, edited by Mark A. Runco and Steven R. Pritzker (San Diego, CA: Academic Press, 1999) 403–412.

Scott G. Isaksen, Kenneth J. Lauer, and Göran Ekvall, "Situational Outlook Questionnaire: A Measure of the Climate for Creativity and Change," Psychological Reports 1999, 85: 665–674.

4   Top Five Climate Dimensions - If you want to dig into a relatively engaging textbook on the ins and outs of organizational creativity, I highly recommend: Gerard J. Puccio, John F. Cabra, and Nathan Schwagler, Organizational Creativity: A Practical Guide for Innovators and Entrepreneurs (Los Angeles, CA: Sage, 2018).

Chapter 11

1   Universal Creative Process - This mash-up between
     creative problem solving and design thinking models
     can be found in: Gerard J. Puccio, John F. Cabra,
     and Nathan Schwagler, Organizational Creativity: A
     Practical Guide for Innovators and Entrepreneurs (Los
     Angeles, CA: Sage, 2018).

2   Applied Creativity - Wallas depicted a four-stage
     creative process (Preparation, Incubation, Illumination,
     Verification) in his book: Graham Wallas, The Art
     of Thought (London, UK: Jonathan Cape, 1926).
     In 1953, Alex Osborn originated the seven-step
     Creative Problem Solving (CPS) process (Orientation,
     Preparation, Analysis, Hypothesis, Incubation,
     Synthesis, Verification): Alex Osborn, Applied
     Imagination, (New York: Charles Scribner's Sons, 1953).
     The process has evolved since then, but still has many
     of the elements included by Osborn.

3   Human-Centered Design - IDEO is a leader in bringing
     human-centered design outside the traditional design
     fields. This book is written by the IDEO CEO and
     president about his experience using design thinking
     across industries. Tim Brown, Change by Design:
     How Design Thinking Transforms Organizations and
     Inspires Innovation (New York: HarperBusiness, 2009).

4   IBM Loop - IBM process loop: https://www.ibm.com/
     design/thinking/page/framework/

     Michael Ackerbauer overlay: ibm.biz/agile-innovation

5   Kimberly-Clark - Clayton W. Bunyard, "The Creative
     Thinking Field Book: Putting Creative Problem Solving
     into the Context of Research & Development,"Creative

Studies Graduate Student Masters Projects, 2016, Paper 241. http://digitalcommons.buffalostate.edu/cgi/viewcontent.cgi?article=1248&context=creativeprojects.

6   Thinking Preferences - FourSight is based on rigorous research and field studies. One of the foundational works: Gerard Puccio, "Creative Problem Solving Preferences: Their Identification and Implications", Creativity and Innovation Management 1999: 8, 171–178.

7   IBM Study - IBM internal study: Casimer DeCusatis, "Creating, Growing and Sustaining Efficient Innovation Teams," Creativity and Innovation Management 2008: 17, 155–164. Available at SSRN: https://ssrn.com/abstract=1130525.

8   Cognitive bias/unconscious incompetence - based on research by Charlie Garland of The Innovation Habit: https://theinnovationhabit.com

Chapter 12

1   The Design Squiggle - This an open-source model. Graphic and full story can be found on Damien Newman's site: https://thedesignsquiggle.com.

2   Fake Einstein Quote - Never trust a quote you see on a meme. This is a great site for helping debunk false quotes: https://quoteinvestigator.com/2014/05/22/solve/.

3   Question-Storming - See https://www.fastcompany.com/3060573/how-brainstorming-questions-not-ideas-sparks-creativity and Warren Berger, A More Beautiful Question (New York, NY: Bloomsbury, 2014).

4   Identify Pathways - Adapted from Miller, Vehar, Firestien, Thurber, and Nielsen, Creativity Unbound: An Introduction to Creative Process (5th Ed.), (Evanston, IL: FourSight, LLC, 2011).

5   Side Effects of Brainstorming - Eyman cites six additional benefits of group ideation sessions: consensus building, team building, engagement, motivation, understanding the issue, and post-session ideas. Read the article in: David Eyman, "Are the Other Benefits of Group Creativity Practices Just as Important as Good Ideas?" in Big Questions in Creativity 2015, Mary Kay Culpepper and Cynthia Burnett, eds. (Buffalo: NY, ICSC Press, 2015) 66–77.

6   Brainwriting - Adapted from Roger Firestien, Leading on the Creative Edge (Colorado Springs, CO: Pinon Press, 1996) 96.

7   Creativity Training - Puccio, Burnett, Acar, Yudess, Holinger, and Cabra, "Creative Problem Solving in Small Groups: The Effects of Creativity Training on Idea Generation, Solution Creativity, and Leadership Effectiveness," Journal of Creative Behavior 2019: 1–19. doi:10.1002/jocb.381.

8   Instant Pot - Interesting company story at these links:

      https://ottawacitizen.com/life/food/the-instant-pot-invented-in-ottawa-is-the-hottest-multi-cooker-in-kitchens

      https://www.forbes.com/sites/davidhochman/2018/01/24/instant-pot-inventor-explains-why-the-worlds-gone-mad-for-slow-cooking/#59afadfc7c35

9   Assisters and Resisters - Adapted from Noller, Parnes, and Biondi, Creative Actionbook (New York: Scribner's Sons, 1976).

10   Take Action - Adapted from Miller, Vehar, Firestien, Thurber, and Nielsen, Creativity Unbound: An Introduction to Creative Process (5th Ed.), (Evanston, IL: FourSight, LLC, 2011).

Chapter 13

1   Metrics - Tristan Kromer, "Metrics for Measuring Innovation Health," Innov8trs Miami, 21 February 2019. Link: https://www.kromatic.com.

2   Creative Product Analysis Model - Susan Besemer, "Creative Product Analysis Matrix: Testing the Model Structure and a Comparison Among Products – Three Novel Chairs," Creativity Research Journal 1998, 11:333-346. Link: https://alicarnold.wordpress.com/cpss/.

Author Biography

Kathryn Haydon, MSc, is a creativity and innovation strategist, skilled facilitator, and keynote speaker with over two decades of experience maximizing individual and collaborative creativity. She trains individuals, leaders, and teams with the tools they need to embrace change with confidence and think up the next big idea, consistently.

An award-winning educator, Kathryn has written and spoken widely on creative learning and the secret strengths of outlier learners. She co-authored *Creativity for Everybody* (2015) and *Discovering and Developing Talents in Spanish Speaking Students* (2012); and she has written several chapters in edited volumes. Kathryn has written extensively for educational journals and publications including *Psychology Today,* Penguin Random House's *Brightly,* and *The Creativity Post.* Her writing has appeared in *The Washington Post.*

Kathryn earned her BA in Spanish literature and culture, with a minor in economics, at Northwestern University, and her MSc in creativity and change leadership from the acclaimed International Center for Studies in Creativity at SUNY, Buffalo.

Index